Bridge Sleuth

Bridge Sleuth

Who Has What?

JOE BLATNICK

authorHOUSE®

AuthorHouse™
1663 Liberty Drive
Bloomington, IN 47403
www.authorhouse.com
Phone: 1 (800) 839-8640

Published by AuthorHouse 12/18/2015

ISBN: 978-1-5049-5591-1 (sc)
ISBN: 978-1-5049-5592-8 (e)

Print information available on the last page.

This book is printed on acid-free paper.

BRIDGE SLEUTH
WHO has WHAT?

About the Author

Although Joe, at the young age of 80, has entered a semi-retired state, as it applies to bridge activities, his involvement in the game continues. Teaching locally and on high seas has ended but the writing continues. The published books are 5 in total with more in various stages of completion.

Introduction

As the title of this book implies, it will guide the reader down the same path which most experienced players follow. The art of counting and card reading – synonymous terms – thought to be the exclusive domain of experts will, if the reader puts in a little effort become second nature. As this state begins to take shape, it will seem that a door has been opened or the trees in the forest have suddenly parted and the path is clear.

Although, to the newer players, the success of the better players seems to be 'luck' rather than anything else, this is only partially true. In assuming a certain lie of the cards, often a necessity if success is to be achieved, luck does enter the picture. However, there has been a great deal of planning involved in reaching the lucky stage. An old adage comes to mind, "The harder I work, the luckier I get".

It is the better players' ability to visualize certain holdings, not peeking or gamesmanship which leads to success. These better players gather clues from the bidding, the opening lead, along with the subsequent play and then plan accordingly.

Although said players are able to execute those exotic techniques such as end plays, squeezes and coups, it is their gathering of these clues and subsequent planning which has led to success, and to the untrained eye, seem so difficult.

Read on and become one of these seemingly exalted types.

Preface

It has been said that bidding is the most important part of bridge. I like to say that bidding is 75% of the game with the other 25% being bidding. No, you've not just seen a misprint. Bidding is that important to one's success. Get the bidding right and other aspects of the game will follow. That having been said, let's not overlook the importance played by proper technique as applied to declarer play.

Lack of planning, mishandling common card combinations and general laziness all play an integral part in the failure of many.

Depending on the contract, N.T. or a suit, counting winners or losers as soon as dummy hits the table is an absolute necessity. Yet how many times have you seen an opponent (never you, of course) call a card from dummy immediately?

When it comes to handling those common card combinations, here are just three, which are commonly mishandled.

> 1. Qxx   Try not to lead this suit. As soon as your opponents do, they've
>   Jxx   handed you a trick.
>
> 2. AJ9   Unless you have evidence to the contrary, lead low and finesse
>   xxx   the 9.
>
> 3. Kx   If possible, win the first trick with the King and then keep the
>   Qxx   opponent on your right off lead.

The laziness issue comes into play frequently. You must be constantly vigilant and yet most of us can't always be bothered.

Pay attention to those seemingly tedious tasks and reap the benefits.

Table of Contents

Declarer Play

Defence

Questions for Declarer

1. A Long Minor for N.T.

Dummy
- ♠ 72
- ♥ J103
- ♦ AK97532
- ♣ 9

West leads the ♥7, Jack from dummy and you allow East's Queen to hold. East now leads the ♣Ace, followed by the 4. How do you proceed?

```
        N
   W         E
        S
```

- ♠ AK85 (you)
- ♥ A64
- ♦ 86
- ♣ KJ105

E/W Vul.

West	North	East	South
		1♥	1N.T
P	3N.T.	P	

Opening Lead: ♥7

Ask Yourself
1. How many points does West have?
2. Who has the ♣Ace?
3. Where is the ♥King?
4. Who is the dangerous opponent?
5. How many hearts does West have left?
6. What's your plan?

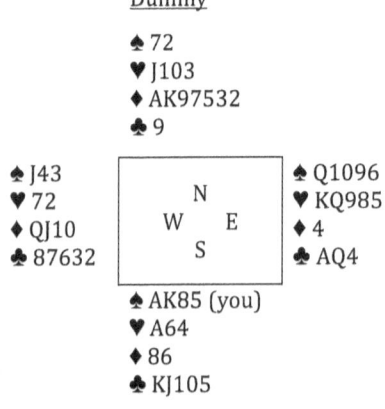

Dummy
- ♠ 72
- ♥ J103
- ♦ AK97532
- ♣ 9

West
- ♠ J43
- ♥ 72
- ♦ QJ10
- ♣ 87632

East
- ♠ Q1096
- ♥ KQ985
- ♦ 4
- ♣ AQ4

South
- ♠ AK85 (you)
- ♥ A64
- ♦ 86
- ♣ KJ105

Answers
1. Since you and dummy have a total of 23 and East opened the bidding, West cannot have more than 4 or 5.
2. East must have the ♣Ace as part of the opening bid.
3. The ♥King must also be with East. If it was with West, it would have been the opening lead.
4. West is the dangerous opponent because you wouldn't want another heart lead from that side before the diamonds were established.

5. West cannot have more than one heart left. Your side has 6 and East opened that suit, showing at least 5.
6. You can't afford to let West gain the lead before the diamonds are established. Win trick 3 with your ♣King and duck a diamond.

2. Six / Five, Come Alive

Dummy
♠ J72
♥ Q10
♦ A53
♣ A7632

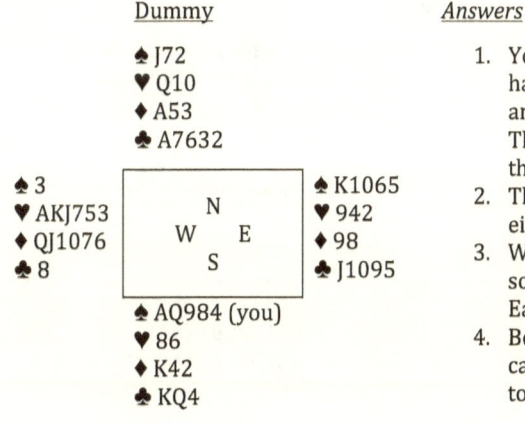

♠ AQ984 (you)
♥ 86
♦ K42
♣ KQ4

E/W Vul.

West	North	East	South
			1♠
2♥	3♣	P	3♠
4♦	4♠		

Opening Lead: ♥Ace

After cashing the Ace and King of hearts, West switched to the ♦Queen. Over to you.

Ask Yourself
1. How many points in East's hand?
2. What is the most likely distribution of the red suits in West's hand?
3. Which of the two opponents has more trump?
4. Who is more likely to have the ♠King?
5. Why must you assume that West has a singleton trump?
6. How many clubs could West have?
7. How should you proceed?

Dummy
♠ J72
♥ Q10
♦ A53
♣ A7632

♠ 3
♥ AKJ753
♦ QJ1076
♣ 8

♠ K1065
♥ 942
♦ 98
♣ J1095

♠ AQ984 (you)
♥ 86
♦ K42
♣ KQ4

Answers
1. You and dummy have 25. West has made two bids and must have an opening hand or close to it. Therefore East cannot have more than 3 or 4.
2. The red suits in West's hand are either 6 – 6, 6 - 5 or 5 – 5.
3. West has only 2 or 3 black cards, so must have fewer spades than East.
4. Because East has more black cards, East is therefore most likely to have the ♠King.

5. If West's black cards were all clubs, East would have too many spades for you to overcome.
6. If you assume that West has a singleton spade, depending on the distribution of the red suits, West could have 0, 1 or 2 clubs.

3

3. Double Fit

♠ 432
♥ 432
♦ QJ653
♣ 105

If it hasn't been drawn to your attention before, this hand will certainly make it clear – fits, not H.C.P. take tricks. This hand will take 12 tricks on only 29 H.C.P.

♠ AQ (you)
♥ AQJ107
♦ AK4
♣ AQ2

Both Vul.

West	North	East	South
1♠	P	P	Dbl.
P	4♥	P	3♥
P			

Ask Yourself

1. How many points does East have?
2. What's your plan?

Opening Lead: ♠Jack

Dummy

♠ 432
♥ 432
♦ QJ653
♣ 105

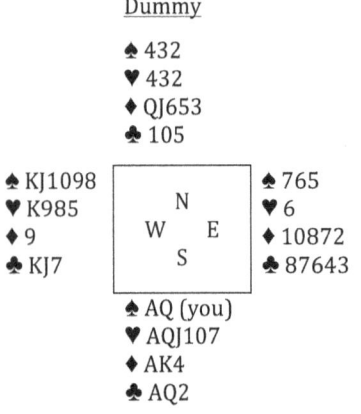

♠ KJ1098
♥ K985
♦ 9
♣ KJ7

♠ 765
♥ 6
♦ 10872
♣ 87643

♠ AQ (you)
♥ AQJ107
♦ AK4
♣ AQ2

Answers

1. East cannot have any H.C.P. West opened with no Aces and must therefore have all the missing honours.
2. Counting your tricks reveals 2 spades, 4 hearts, 5 diamonds and one club. Since West has all the missing honours, you know that any finesse is doomed, simply take trick #1 with the Queen, lay down the trump Ace and concede the trump King to West. Win any return, finish drawing trump and run the diamonds. Don't lament

missing the slam. Had West chosen to lead the singleton diamond rather than a spade which provided you with a free finesse, you couldn't have taken more than 11 tricks.

4. Extra Winners

<u>Dummy</u>
♠ 4
♥ A10
♦ AK432
♣ A9876

♠ AKQ8632 (you)
♥ 7
♦ Q5
♣ 543

You take dummy's Ace while East contributes the 10. When you cash two high trump, West is revealed to have a trump trick. You must eliminate both club losers.

N/S Vul.

West	North	East	South
			1♠
P	2♦	3♥	3♠
P	4♣	P	4♠
P	6♠		

Opening Lead: ♣King

<u>Ask Yourself</u>
1. Who has the club Queen and Jack?
2. How many clubs in East's hand? How many hearts? Diamonds?
3. What's your plan?

<u>Dummy</u>
♠ 4
♥ A10
♦ AK432
♣ A9876

♠ 10975   ♠ J
♥ 652   ♥ QJ109843
♦ J108   ♦ 976
♣ KQJ   ♣ 102

♠ AKQ8632 (you)
♥ 7
♦ Q5
♣ 543

<u>Answers</u>
1. The Queen and Jack of clubs are with West. It sure looks like East's play of the 10 on the first trick was the top of a doubleton.
2. East likely has 7 hearts for the pre-emptive overcall and with a singleton spade and 2 clubs must have 3 diamonds.
3. After cashing a third trump, play 4 rounds of diamonds, pitching both club losers. West can trump that 4th round but that will be the defences' only trick – a loser on loser.

5

5. Help From the Helpless

<u>Dummy</u>
♠ KQ75
♥ 865
♦ Q64
♣ K85

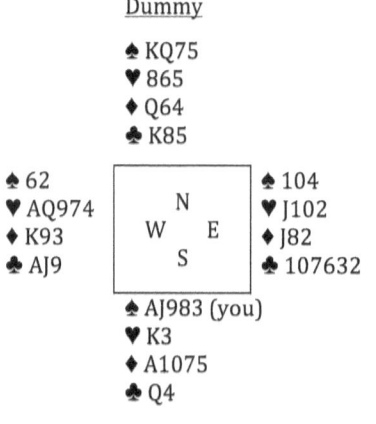

♠ AJ983 (you)
♥ K3
♦ A1075
♣ Q4

Both Vul.

West	North	East	South
			1♠
Dbl.	3♦*	P	4♠

Opening Lead: ♠6

*This is the Bergen raise – 10 to 12 pts. and at least 4 spades in support.
Not wanting to lead from tenaces in the rounded suits nor the ♦King, West chose a passive trump lead.

Ask Yourself

1. How many points in West's hand?
2. How many losers do you have?
3. How could you get West to help you eliminate one of them?
4. Should you draw trump first?
5. What then?

<u>Dummy</u>
♠ KQ75
♥ 865
♦ Q64
♣ K85

♠ 62		♠ 104
♥ AQ974	N	♥ J102
♦ K93	W E	♦ J82
♣ AJ9	S	♣ 107632

♠ AJ983 (you)
♥ K3
♦ A1075
♣ Q4

Answers

1. Having doubled for take-out, West has most of the missing points. The best East could have is 2 Jacks or a Jack and a Queen.
2. In a worst case scenario you would have 5 – 2 hearts, 2 diamonds and a club. However, since East can't have the ♦King, it's really only 4.
3. You could enlist West's help with an elimination and throw-in.
4. Absolutely. That's part of the elimination. It also prevents an unexpected ruff.
5. After drawing trump, lead towards the ♦Queen. West will win the King. Win the diamond return and lead a club towards dummy. When the King wins, cash 3 diamonds, pitching a club from dummy and lead the ♣Queen. West will win but is saddled with a Hobson's

6

choice – lead a heart, making your King into a winner or lead a club allowing you to ruff in dummy while discarding a heart. In the end, your losers are a heart, a diamond, and a club.

6. Another Helpful Defender

<u>Dummy</u>
♠ KQ76
♥ AJ1053
♦ J10
♣ Q2

```
      N
  W       E
      S
```

♠ 854 (you)
♥ KQ642
♦ 8
♣ AJ73

N/S Vul.

West	North	East	South
1♦	Dbl.	3♦	3♥
P	4♥		

Opening Lead: ♦Ace

On trick #2 you ruff the ♦King. Now what?

Ask Yourself
1. What is the likely division of points between defenders?
2. What important cards do the opponents hold?
3. What is the most logical division of these important honours?
4. Should you be leading first towards the ♣Queen or ♠K/Q?

<u>Dummy</u>
♠ KQ76
♥ AJ1053
♦ J10
♣ Q2

♠ 1092		♠ AJ3
♥ 8	N	♥ 97
♦ AKQ64	W E	♦ 97532
♣ K964	S	♣ 1085

♠ 854 (you)
♥ KQ642
♦ 8
♣ AJ73

Answers
1. West opened and East made a pre-emptive raise and should have 5 or 6 points. Since West needs enough to open, West's hand must have 12 or 13.
2. & 3. Since the defenders have the A/J of spades and ♣King, it would seem that East has the A/J of spades and West the ♣King. No other combinations of these 3 honours seem plausible.
4. By trying the clubs first you would subsequently be able to discard 2 of dummy's spades on your good clubs. West will take the King on the first club lead for fear of losing it to a ruff.

7. How Selfish

<u>Dummy</u>
♠ KQ
♥ QJ72
♦ A98
♣ 9642

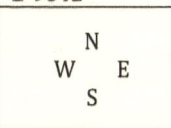

♠ AJ10843 (you)
♥ 10
♦ KJ7
♣ QJ10

Neither Vul.

West	North	East	South
1N.T.	P	P	2♠
P	4♠		

Opening Lead: ♥Ace

After the discouraging 3 from partner on the opening lead, West switches to a trump. How do you continue?

Ask Yourself

1. Where are all defenders' points?
2. How many losers do you have?
3. What's your plan for eliminating one of them?

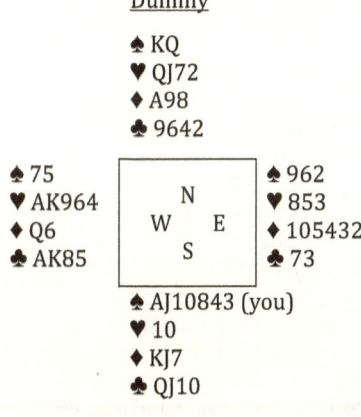

<u>Dummy</u>
♠ KQ
♥ QJ72
♦ A98
♣ 9642

♠ 75
♥ AK964
♦ Q6
♣ AK85

♠ 962
♥ 853
♦ 105432
♣ 73

♠ AJ10843 (you)
♥ 10
♦ KJ7
♣ QJ10

Answers

1. Since West opened 1N.T., East would be lucky to have a Jack. Selfish West has them all.
2. You have 4 possible losers – the heart already lost, two immediate clubs and an eventual diamond.
3. Upon drawing all the trump, lead a club. West will win and is immediately end played. West could cash a second club but that would be the third and last trick for the defence as you could eventually discard a losing diamond on dummy ♣9. If instead, West led a diamond, that would eliminate your diamond loser. If West tried to cash a second heart, you could trump, enter dummy with a diamond and discard your diamond loser on the established heart. If West led a small heart you could win in dummy while discarding that same diamond loser.

Imagine! Endplaying an opponent so early in the play.

9

8. Similarly Revealing

Dummy
♠ A102
♥ Q73
♦ KQ86
♣ Q84

♠ K3 (you)
♥ K
♦ AJ97542
♣ A93

1. Strong hand.
2. Balanced hand, bid something partner.
3. Diamonds accepted as trump, showing first round control.
4. Also showing first round control.

You win the opening lead with your King. Now what?

West	North	East	South
1♥	Dbl.*	P	2♥[1]
P	2N.T.[2]	P	3♦
P	3♠[3]	P	4♣[4]
P	6♦		

Ask Yourself
1. Who has all of the 12 missing points?
2. How many losers do you have?
3. What's your plan?

Opening Lead: ♠Queen

*This is a bad take-out double. Doubling a major, for take-out, demands that you have 4 cards in the other major.

Dummy
♠ A102
♥ Q73
♦ KQ86
♣ Q84

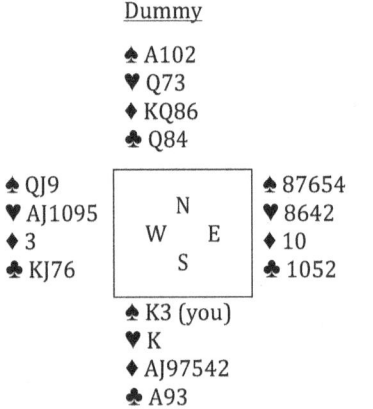

♠ QJ9
♥ AJ1095
♦ 3
♣ KJ76

♠ 87654
♥ 8642
♦ 10
♣ 1052

♠ K3 (you)
♥ K
♦ AJ97542
♣ A93

Answers
1. It doesn't take much effort to determine that West has all of them. As if West's bid wasn't enough to allow your placing of all missing honours, the lead of the ♠Queen confirms that East can't even have the ♠Jack.
2. You have two potential losers in clubs and an obvious one in hearts.
3. Win the opening lead with your ♠King, draw trump and lead your ♠3. By finessing the ♠10 you are able to discard your singleton

heart on dummy ♠Ace. You can subsequently lead a club towards dummy's Queen and eliminate a club loser. You will eventually lose only the one club and make your slam. Alternatively, you could get rid of one club on the extra spade (after the successful finesse) and the second club on dummy's ♥Queen.

9. Ah, Deception

Dummy
♠ AJ2
♥ 752
♦ J874
♣ K63

♠ 54 (you)
♥ J1093
♦ AKQ5
♣ AQ10

Both Vul.

West	North	East	South
P	P	P	1N.T.
P	2N.T.	P	3N.T.

Opening Lead: ♥Ace*

*Standard practice when partner opens with an Ace against 3N.T. is to drop an honour if you have one. Failing that your obligation is to give count. A high card shows an even number, a low one showing an odd number.

When East plays the 6, drop your ten.

Ask Yourself

1. What will your ♥10 accomplish?
2. How many top tricks do you have?
3. Where will one more materialize?

Dummy

♠ AJ2
♥ 752
♦ J874
♣ K63

♠ 10963   ♠ KQ87
♥ AKQ8   N   ♥ 64
♦ 3   W   E   ♦ 10962
♣ J852   S   ♣ 974

♠ 54 (you)
♥ J1093
♦ AKQ5
♣ AQ10

Answers

1. By dropping your ten you are hoping that West will place East with the 9-6-4-3. East's play of the 6 would be consistent with someone showing a even number of cards but not wanting to waste the 9. This will cause West to continue hearts instead of possibly switching to a spade which would be most unwelcome.

2. You have 8 top tricks – one spade, 4 diamonds and 3 clubs.

3. If West is taken in by your ruse on trick one, your ninth trick will be a heart.

10. A Dead Giveaway

<u>Dummy</u>
♠ AQ1042
♥ K753
♦ 109
♣ A3

```
      N
  W       E
      S
```

♠ KJ953 (you)
♥ QJ6
♦ Q74
♣ Q8

Neither Vul.

West	North	East	South
1♣	Dbl.	P	2♠
3♦	4♠		

Opening Lead: ♦Ace

On the ♦Ace, East plays a discouraging 2. If East had a doubleton a higher card would have been played. Not wanting to establish Declarer's ♦Queen, West shifts to a trump on trick #2.

Ask Yourself
1. Does East have any points?
2. Why?
3. How many losers do you have?
4. How can you eliminate one of them?

<u>Dummy</u>
♠ AQ1042
♥ K753
♦ 109
♣ A3

♠ 8
♥ A
♦ AKJ85
♣ KJ10742

```
      N
  W       E
      S
```

♠ 76
♥ 109843
♦ 632
♣ 965

♠ KJ953 (you)
♥ QJ6
♦ Q74
♣ Q8

Answers
1. & 2. East doesn't likely have any points since West reversed by bidding clubs first and following with diamonds. This requires at least 17 points.
3. You have 4 losers – one club, 2 diamonds and a heart. However, the club loser is not of the immediate type. You have time to get rid of it.
4. Win trick #2 and take a second round of trump finishing in your hand. Now lead a small heart towards the King. When the Ace appears immediately, you have found a parking spot for your club loser – dummy's ♥King.

11. A Simple One

*5-5 in the minors

Dummy
- ♠ AQ109
- ♥ KQ976
- ♦ K2
- ♣ 54

*5-5 in the minors

You play low from dummy on the first trick and take East's Jack with your King.

```
      N
  W       E
      S
```

- ♠ K72 (you)
- ♥ AJ1043
- ♦ AJ5
- ♣ K7

N/S Vul.

West	North	East	South
---	---	---	1♥
2N.T.*	3♠	P	3N.T.
P	4♣	P	4♠
P	6♥		

Ask Yourself
1. How many losers do you have?
2. Do you have any extra winners?
3. What's your plan?

Opening Lead: ♠6

Dummy
- ♠ AQ109
- ♥ KQ976
- ♦ K2
- ♣ 54

♠ 65		♠ J843
♥ 2	N	♥ 85
♦ Q10943	W E	♦ 876
♣ AQJ106	S	♣ 9832

- ♠ K72 (you)
- ♥ AJ1043
- ♦ AJ5
- ♣ K7

Answers

1. You have two potential losers, both in clubs.
2. Because the opening lead enabled you to pick up the ♠Jack, you have an extra winner in spades.
3. After drawing trump, simply lead a spade to dummy and on the fourth spade discard a club. Now you only have one club loser – mission accomplished.
   Although leading a singleton trump is normally a losing strategy, in this case it would have made declarer's task a little more difficult.

13

12. Scissors Coup

<u>Dummy</u>
♠ 965
♥ 872
♦ AQ43
♣ AK6

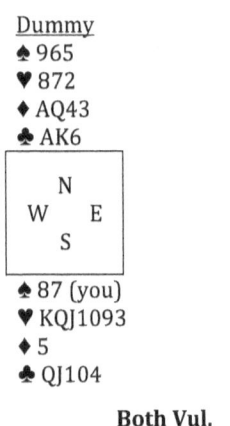

♠ 87 (you)
♥ KQJ1093
♦ 5
♣ QJ104

Both Vul.

West	North	East	South
---	---	1♠	2♥
2♠	4♥		

Opening Lead: ♠King

East overtakes the opening lead and returns the ♣5.

Ask Yourself
1. Why would East overtake the opening lead and return the club.
2. Who has the trump Ace?
3. How many losers do you have?
4. Where's the danger?
5. Where's the ♦King?
6. How can you prevail?

<u>Dummy</u>
♠ 965
♥ 872
♦ AQ43
♣ AK6

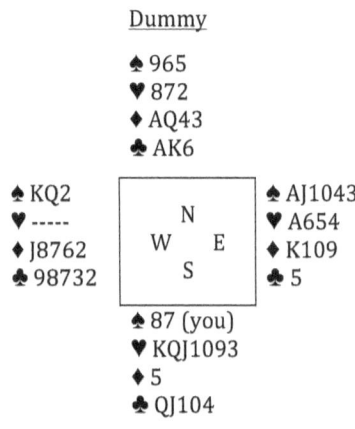

♠ KQ2   ♠ AJ1043
♥ -----   ♥ A654
♦ J8762   ♦ K109
♣ 98732   ♣ 5

♠ 87 (you)
♥ KQJ1093
♦ 5
♣ QJ104

Answers
1. & 2. There can be no other reason for East's apparently strange play except that the club is a singleton and East is looking for a ruff. This can only occur if West can be put on lead while East still has trump left. And such a precise scenario can only be accomplished if East can take an early trump trick – the Ace.
3. Things look rosy with only 3 losers – a heart and 2 spades.
4. East will win the trump Ace, put partner on lead with the ♠Queen and get the club ruff.
5. East was the opener so must have the ♦King for the necessary values. So you can forget about a diamond finesse to allow you to pitch a spade.
6. Win trick #2 in dummy, cash the ♦Ace and on the ♦Queen throw your remaining spade. Now East will be unable to reach West by leading a spade.

13. Take Care

<u>Dummy</u>
♠ J54
♥ 83
♦ A1072
♣ 9876

```
      N
  W       E
      S
```

♠ AKQ1098 (you)
♥ K7
♦ 8
♣ AKQ5

You take the opening lead with the King. This might convince West that East has the Queen. It never hurts to muddy the waters.

N/S Vul.

West	North	East	South
---	---	---	2♣
P	2♦	2♥	2♠
P	3♠	P	4N.T.
P	5♣	P	6♠

Opening Lead: ♣J

Ask Yourself
1. Why the club lead by West?
2. Where is the ♥Ace?
3. What's the club situation?
4. How are the missing spades likely divided?
5. Is there a potential problem?
6. What's your plan?

<u>Dummy</u>
♠ J54
♥ 83
♦ A1072
♣ 9876

```
♠ 632          ♠ 7
♥ 9542    N    ♥ AQJ106
♦ J6543  W   E ♦ KQ9
♣ J       S    ♣ 10432
```

♠ AKQ1098 (you)
♥ K7
♦ 8
♣ AKQ5

Answers
1. The opening lead is obviously a singleton. Why else would West choose not to lead partner's suit.
2. The ♥Ace can only be with East. When an opponent opens 2♣, the only reason for entering the fray is lead-directing.
3. East has 4 clubs to the ten, making it finessable if a finesse is needed.
4. Since East bid hearts and has shown up with 4 clubs, East's hand has only 4 unknown cards. West has at least 3 hearts and a singleton club so has more unknown cards. West could have 4 spades or only 3.
5. You need to finesse the club through East as well as lead towards your ♥King. Therefore you need 2 entries to dummy. You have them in the ♠Jack and ♦Ace.

6. Win the first trick and play 3 rounds of trump, ending in dummy. It doesn't matter whether you make the heart or club play first. Make the other one when you re-enter dummy with the diamond.

14. Nowhere to Hide

Dummy
♠ 754
♥ KQ43
♦ AKQ5
♣ K8

```
      N
  W       E
      S
```

♠ AK98 (you)
♥ A62
♦ 874
♣ AQ9

Neither Vul.

West	North	East	South
---	---	---	1N.T.
P	6N.T.		

Opening Lead: ♠Queen

East discards a club on the opening lead.

Ask Yourself

1. How many winners do you have?
2. Where might you get another?
3. How many spades did West have to start?
4. How many unknown cards in West's hand?
5. Now what?

Dummy

♠ 754
♥ KQ43
♦ AKQ5
♣ K8

♠ QJ10632		♠ -----
♥ 95	N	♥ J1087
♦ 63	W E	♦ J1092
♣ 1075	S	♣ J6432

♠ AK98 (you)
♥ A62
♦ 874
♣ AQ9

Answers

1. You have eleven winners – 2 spades, 3 hearts, 3 diamonds and 3 clubs.
2. Hopefully one of your red suits will break 3-3, giving you your twelfth trick.
3. Since East showed out on the first trick, West must have started with 6 spades.
4. West has 7 unknown cards.
5. You are one trick short of your goal. Start by cashing the winners in your red suits after winning the first trick. It may be your lucky day – one of them might break favourably, producing your twelfth trick. If neither does and if your luck is as bad as mine, neither will. Now cash 3 clubs, producing this position.

<u>West</u>
J106

      <u>You</u>
      A98

Lead a low spade and West will be West of a rock and East of a hard place.

15. Assumption

Dummy
- ♠ AQ62
- ♥ 984
- ♦ J10
- ♣ AQ95

```
      N
  W       E
      S
```

- ♠ KJ43 (you)
- ♥ 75
- ♦ KQ2
- ♣ J864

Both Vul.

West	North	East	South
---	---	1♥	P
P	Dbl.	P	1♠
P	3♠	P	4♠

Opening Lead: ♥Queen

Although North's bidding wouldn't meet with universal approval, the play is the thing. You ruff the third heart and draw 3 rounds of trump, East showing up with 3.

Ask Yourself
1. Who has the ♦Ace? The ♣King?
2. How many losers do you have?
3. How do you eliminate one of them?

Dummy
- ♠ AQ62
- ♥ 984
- ♦ J10
- ♣ AQ95

♠ 87
♥ QJ10
♦ 8643
♣ 10732

```
      N
  W       E
      S
```

♠ 1095
♥ AK632
♦ A975
♣ K

- ♠ KJ43 (you)
- ♥ 75
- ♦ KQ2
- ♣ J864

Answers

1. West has already shown up with the Q/J/10 of hearts. Had that hand also held the ♦Ace or ♣King, it would have raised partner.
2. You have 4 losers – the 2 hearts already lost plus a club and diamond.
3. You know that East has the ♣King. You must assume that it is a singleton. Play dummy's ♣Ace and when the King falls, just adopt a casual look as though you knew it all along. However, your brilliance hasn't ended the play. You still have to come back to your hand and finesse against West's ♣10. Once again you've covered up for partner's exuberance.

16. A Powerhouse

Dummy
♠ 10632
♥ 10975
♦ Q52
♣ A8

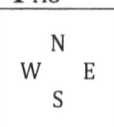

♠ AKQ (you)
♥ AKQ
♦ AK93
♣ K97

Neither Vul.

West	North	East	South
---	---	---	3N.T.
P	6N.T.		

Opening Lead: ♣Queen

The 3N.T. opening promises 28 pts. and with 6, North is happy to raise to 6. The opening club lead certainly looks like the top of a sequence. Just in case you need both dummy entries later, take trick one with your King.

Ask Yourself
1. How many quick tricks do you have?
2. Where might you produce one more?
3. What's your hope?
4. What's your plan if your hopes are dashed?

Dummy
♠ 10632
♥ 10975
♦ Q52
♣ A8

♠ 54   ♠ J987
♥ J862   ♥ 43
♦ J764   ♦ 108
♣ QJ10   ♣ 86542

♠ AKQ (you)
♥ AKQ
♦ AK93
♣ K97

Answers
1. You have eleven tricks there for the taking – 3 spades, 3 hearts, 3 diamonds and 2 clubs.
2. & 3. To produce one more trick you can hope that one of your 7 card suits breaks 3-3.
4. As is your lot in life, your hopes are dashed and you must look elsewhere for that slam fulfilling trick. As you cashed that A/K/Q in spades, hearts and diamonds, West showed 2 spades, 4 hearts, 4 diamonds and 3 clubs. These were everyone's last 3 cards. When you

                    ♥ 10
                    ♦ 10
                    ♣ A
♥ J   ♠ J
♦ J   ♣ 86
♣ J

                    ♠ 3
                    ♣ 97

lead the ♠3, West let's go of the ♣ and you pitch dummy's Ace. East wins and has to lead into your club tenace. This was not the 'Devil's Coup' per se but you must have had a pact with the horned one to pull this off.

17. Protect Your Winners

Dummy
- ♠ 643
- ♥ 104
- ♦ KQJ
- ♣ AJ752

- ♠ A9 (you)
- ♥ AKJ3
- ♦ 1098652
- ♣ 6

Neither Vul.

West	North	East	South
			1♦
P	2♣	P	2♥
P	4♦	P	5♦

Opening Lead: ♠5

East plays the Queen on the opening lead and you win your Ace. Now you cash the hearts and ruff the third, establishing your Jack. When you lead a high diamond, it holds.

Ask Yourself

1. How many losers did you have originally?
2. How many do you have now?
3. Where's the danger?

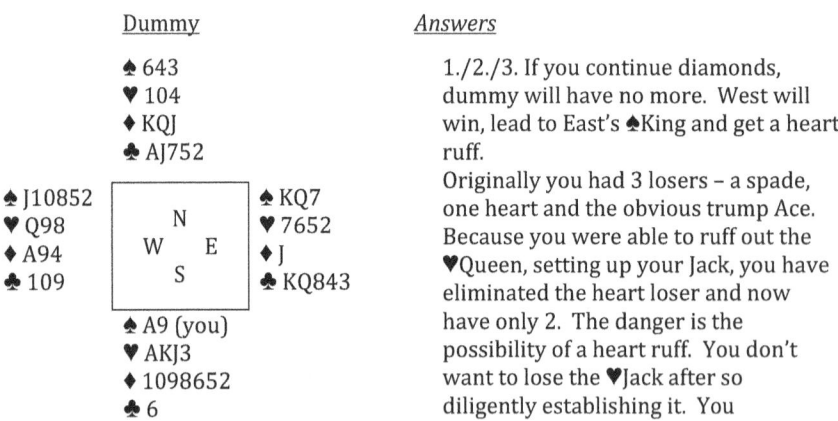

Dummy
- ♠ 643
- ♥ 104
- ♦ KQJ
- ♣ AJ752

West
- ♠ J10852
- ♥ Q98
- ♦ A94
- ♣ 109

East
- ♠ KQ7
- ♥ 7652
- ♦ J
- ♣ KQ843

South
- ♠ A9 (you)
- ♥ AKJ3
- ♦ 1098652
- ♣ 6

Answers

1./2./3. If you continue diamonds, dummy will have no more. West will win, lead to East's ♠King and get a heart ruff.

Originally you had 3 losers – a spade, one heart and the obvious trump Ace. Because you were able to ruff out the ♥Queen, setting up your Jack, you have eliminated the heart loser and now have only 2. The danger is the possibility of a heart ruff. You don't want to lose the ♥Jack after so diligently establishing it. You can overcome this possible disaster by leading a spade from dummy after your ♦King is allowed to win. You were going to lose a spade in any event. By losing it now, you have severed the link to East's hand and the only entry to it. The heart ruff is no longer an issue. You make 5 diamonds, the only losers being the spade and trump Ace.

18. Such Largesse

Dummy
♠ Q
♥ KQ84
♦ AK972
♣ Q93

```
      N
  W       E
      S
```

♠ A1096542 (you)
♥ 63
♦ 6
♣ K106

On the opening lead, East takes dummy's Queen and returns the ♣5. You duck, West wins with the Ace and returns a club, East contributing the 2, confirming a doubleton.

Both Vul.

West	North	East	South
---	1♦	P	1♠
P	2♥	P	2♠
P	2N.T.	P	4♠

Opening Lead: ♥Jack

Ask Yourself

1. How many losers do you have?
2. Where are they?
3. Where's the danger?
4. How do you handle the trump suit?
5. What must you do after winning trick #3 and before tackling trump?

Dummy

♠ Q
♥ KQ84
♦ AK972
♣ Q93

♠ K73   ♠ J8
♥ J109   ♥ A752
♦ J5   ♦ Q10843
♣ AJ874   ♣ 52

```
      N
  W       E
      S
```

♠ A1096542 (you)
♥ 63
♦ 6
♣ K106

Answers

1. There could be as few as 3 or as many as 5, depending on how you handle the black suits.
2. One or two trump, a heart, a club and possibly a club ruff.
3. The danger is allowing East to get the club ruff.
4. The best way to handle this trump combination is to run the Queen.
5. After winning trick #3, immediately cash the high diamonds, discarding your club winner. Such extravagance is necessary to prevent the ruff. After this, you can draw trump – fortunately the Jack

falls. This series of plays limits your losers to one trump, a heart and a club.

19. Show-off

<u>Dummy</u>
♠ 5
♥ AK43
♦ 72
♣ KQJ862

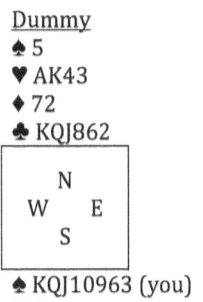

♠ KQJ10963 (you)
♥ 8
♦ Q954
♣ A

N/S Vul.

West	North	East	South
---	1♣	P	1♠
P	2♥	P	2♠
P	3♣	P	4♠

Opening Lead: ♥Queen

The opening lead puts you in dummy for the first and last time. You must be ready for this flamboyant play. Has the title or this preamble made you sit up and take notice.

Ask Yourself
1. How many losers do you have?
2. Can you see the bug in the balm?
3. What's the solution?
4. How many cards, in the critical suit, must East have for this plan to succeed?
5. What will your 10 tricks be?

<u>Dummy</u>
♠ 5
♥ AK43
♦ 72
♣ KQJ862

♠ 42   ♠ A87
♥ QJ7   N   ♥ 109652
♦ AJ63 W E ♦ K108
♣ 9543   S   ♣ 107

♠ KQJ10963 (you)
♥ 8
♦ Q954
♣ A

Answers
1. On the surface, because of dummy's diamond shortage, it would appear that you have only 3 – a trump and 2 diamonds.
2. The bug in the balm or fly in the ointment, if you will, is that there aren't sufficient trump , in dummy, to ruff 2 diamond losers. And when you lead that first diamond, guess what defenders will do.
3. Cash the two high hearts, discarding – are you ready for this – your ♣Ace.
4. The critical suit is clubs and East must have 2.
5. By discarding at least 2 diamonds on the K/Q of clubs, your 10 winners will consist of those 2 clubs, 2 hearts and 6 spades.

20. More Showing-off

Dummy
♠ AK3
♥ 874
♦ QJ6
♣ 8642

♠ ----- (you)
♥ AKQJ652
♦ A85
♣ QJ7

N/S Vul.

West	North	East	South
---	---	1♣	1♥
P	2♥	P	4♥

Opening Lead: ♣10

East takes the first 2 clubs and returns a third, everybody following as you win. You cash a high trump and get the bad news – the ♥8 will no longer be an entry to dummy.

Ask Yourself

1. Do you know the distribution of East's hand?
2. How many points in East's hand?
3. How do you get to dummy and those spade winners?

Dummy
♠ AK3
♥ 874
♦ QJ6
♣ 8642

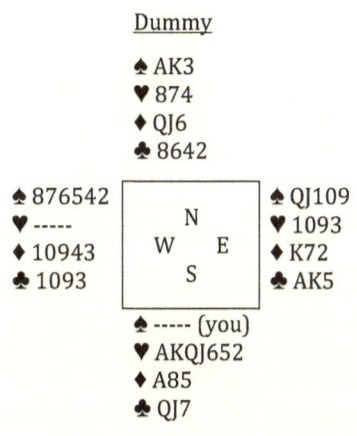

♠ 876542
♥ -----
♦ 10943
♣ 1093

♠ QJ109
♥ 1093
♦ K72
♣ AK5

♠ ----- (you)
♥ AKQJ652
♦ A85
♣ QJ7

Answers

1. East opened a club and therefore had fewer than 5 spades. East has also shown up with 3 clubs and 3 hearts. And if there were 4 diamonds in that hand, the opening would have been 1♦ and not 1♣. Therefore, East's distribution can only be 4 – 3 – 3 – 3.
2. All the missing H.C.P. have to be with East to justify an opening bid. Even if the opening bid had been a stretch, there could only be a Queen or Jack missing from that hand.
3. After the first 3 tricks, all clubs, and the first trump, lead a second trump and then concede a trump to East. East will have nothing but spades or diamonds to lead. A spade lead will allow you to discard 2 diamond losers. A diamond can run around to dummy's Queen, also allowing the discarding of 2 diamonds.

21. Don't Be To Quick

Dummy
♠ J98
♥ AJ
♦ KQ65
♣ J1072

```
        N
    W       E
        S
```

♠ AK1052 (you)
♥ 74
♦ 8
♣ AQ983

West	North	East	South
---	---	---	1♠
P	2♦	P	3♣
P	4♠		

Opening Lead: ♦Jack

If you don't think beyond finesses before looking for another line of play, you'll try both finesses and lose a trick in each suit.

Ask Yourself

1. What is the possible range of points in each defender's hand?
2. Who has the ♦Ace?
3. If East wins trick #1, what will be the likely return?
4. What should you play from dummy on trick #1?
5. How can you avoid one of those losers?

Dummy
♠ J98
♥ AJ
♦ KQ65
♣ J1072

♠ Q3   ♠ 764
♥ K963   ♥ Q10852
♦ J1094   N   ♦ A732
♣ K54   W   E ♣ 6
            S
♠ AK1052 (you)
♥ 74
♦ 8
♣ AQ983

Answers

1. Neither can have more than 10 of their 15 points or you might have heard a bid.
2. It is doubtful that West would lead the Jack, away from the Ace. It must be with East.
3. It will likely be a club, up to dummy's weakness.
4. Duck if you don't want to see a club switch.
5. If West continues with a diamond, cover it and ruff out the Ace. Now you can lead a heart to dummy and discard

your heart loser on the good diamond. Now you can lead dummy's ♠Jack to tempt a cover. When it isn't covered, play the Ace, followed by the King. When the Queen drops, you make an overtrick. Your opponents will think you're just lucky. Partner will be convinced of your genius.

22. One Small Step for Man, A Giant Leap for a Bridge Player

Dummy
♠ J
♥ 762
♦ K954
♣ KQ832

♠ AKQ9843 (you)
♥ A103
♦ AQ3
♣ -----

When you win trick #1 in dummy, you are immediately at the threshold of what is a new experience to many bridge players.

E/W Vul.

West	North	East	South
---	---	1♣	Dbl.
P	1♦	P	2♠
P	3♣	P	6♠

Opening Lead: ♠7

Ask Yourself
1. How many losers do you have?
2. Where are they?
3. Where are all 12 missing points?
4. What do you lead from dummy to trick #2?
5. If East covers, what do you play? And if it isn't?
6. Now what?

Dummy
♠ J
♥ 762
♦ K954
♣ KQ832

♠ 7652   ♠ 10
♥ 9854   ♥ KQJ
♦ 862   ♦ J107
♣ 64   ♣ AJ10975

♠ AKQ9843 (you)
♥ A103
♦ AQ3
♣ -----

Answers
1. & 2. You have 2 losers. Both are hearts.
3. To have come up with an opening bid, East must have all of them.
4. Lead the ♣King.
5. If East covers, discard a heart. If East doesn't cover, you still discard a heart.
6. Even if, by some freak circumstance, you lose this trick to West, you've still unloaded a loser. The other heart loser would go on the established ♣Queen. But be aware. You must resist the

temptation to trump the ♣Ace if East covers. If you were to trump the Ace, the remaining high club in dummy would only allow for the discarding of one heart loser.

23. Believe Thy Opponent

Dummy
♠ 52
♥ A862
♦ KQ10
♣ K1062

♠ Q43 (you)
♥ KQ9
♦ J987
♣ AJ9

Neither Vul.

West	North	East	South
---	---	2♠	P
P	Dbl.	P	2N.T.
P	3N.T.		

Opening Lead: ♠King

East overtakes the opening lead and returns the
♠Jack.

Ask Yourself
1. Why would East overtake the opening lead and continue the suit?
2. What is the only entry card that East could have?
3. Where is the ♣Queen?
4. Which is the danger suit?
5. Which is the only suit which offers any chance of success?
6. How should you handle it.

Dummy

♠ 52
♥ A862
♦ KQ10
♣ K1062

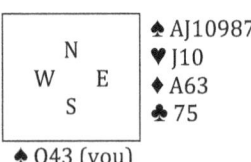

♠ K6   ♠ AJ10987
♥ 7543   ♥ J10
♦ 542   ♦ A63
♣ Q843   ♣ 75

♠ Q43 (you)
♥ KQ9
♦ J987
♣ AJ9

Answers
1. East must be afraid that partner's ♠King is a singleton and wants the suit continued while still in possession of an outside entry.
2. The only possible entry which East could have is the ♦Ace.
3. If the ♣Queen was in East's hand, the hand would have been too strong for a weak 2 opener.
4. Diamonds is the danger suit and must be avoided at all costs.
5. Your only hope lies in clubs.
6. You know the ♣Queen resides with West. Play the Ace and finesse. You'll have one spade, 4 hearts and 4 clubs.

24. Pretend

<u>Dummy</u>
♠ QJ1053
♥ Q85
♦ AJ10
♣ QJ

♠ 62 (you)
♥ AJ10972
♦ KQ
♣ A109

Both Vul.

West	North	East	South
---	---	---	1♥
P	1♠	P	2♥
P	4♥		

Opening Lead: ♠Ace

East contributes the 4 to partner's opening lead.

Ask Yourself
1. Does East want a continuation of spades?
2. How many losers do you have?
3. Where do you get rid of one?
4. What do you contribute to that first trick?

<u>Dummy</u>
♠ QJ1053
♥ Q85
♦ AJ10
♣ QJ

♠ AK7
♥ K3
♦ 7642
♣ K642

♠ 984
♥ 64
♦ 9853
♣ 8753

♠ 62 (you)
♥ AJ10972
♦ KQ
♣ A109

Answers
1. East has no interest in spades being continued. That's why the 4 – lowest card – was played to that first trick.
2. You have four losers – 2 spades, a heart and a club.
3. & 4. You could discard 2 clubs on a spade and diamond winner. Try a little deception. Play your 6 on the opening lead. This will look like East was beginning an echo with the 4/2. You'll lose a second spade trick but you'll be able to discard

one club loser on the ♠Queen and a second on the extra diamond winner in dummy. Your only losers will then be the 2 spades and a trump. When you want a defender to continue the suit being led pretend that defender is your partner and signal accordingly.

25. Be an Explorer

<u>Dummy</u>
♠ K983
♥ AQ72
♦ 4
♣ AJ75

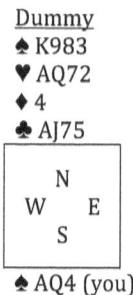

♠ AQ4 (you)
♥ KJ983
♦ KQ5
♣ K6

E/W Vul.

West	North	East	South
---	1♣	2♦	2♥
P	3♥	P	4N.T.
P	5♠	P	6N.T.

Opening Lead: ♦3

Although 6 hearts would be a much safer contract, South being a duplicate player opted for 6N.T. The extra 10 pts. coming from 6N.T. as opposed to hearts is invaluable in duplicate. You win the opening lead with your Queen.

Ask Yourself
1. How many top tricks do you have?
2. What are they?
3. Are any more available? Where?
4. Which suit(s) should you attack first? Why?

<u>Dummy</u>
♠ K983
♥ AQ72
♦ 4
♣ AJ75

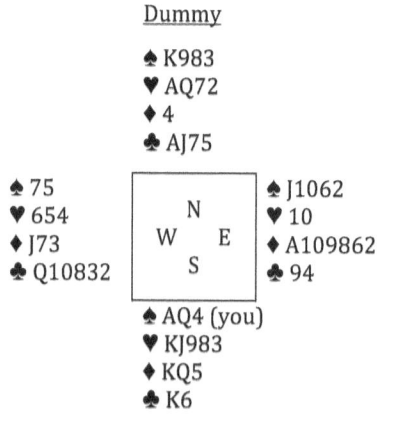

♠ AQ4 (you)
♥ KJ983
♦ KQ5
♣ K6

Answers

1. & 2. You have 11 top tricks. They are the diamond already won, 3 spades, 5 hearts and 2 clubs.
3. You might get a fourth spade if the suit broke 3/3. A successful club finesse could also provide your twelfth trick. Unfortunately, the dummy has no more diamonds or a lead towards your remaining diamond honour could also have done the trick. Ugh!
4. Lead out all your winners in the major suits. If the spades do divide favourably, you'll have 12 tricks. If they don't, you'll at least get a

count. By this discovery play, East's distribution will be revealed as 4 – 1 – 6 – 2. East will be left with the ♠Jack, ♦Ace and ♣9 as the last 3 cards. It will now be a simple matter to cash the ♣King, guarding against East's last club being the Queen, and finesse to bring home an ambitious contract.

26. Convince Your Opponent

Dummy
- ♠ QJ
- ♥ Q5
- ♦ 9843
- ♣ KJ972

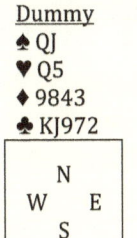

- ♠ K1042 (you)
- ♥ K763
- ♦ K7
- ♣ AQ5

West	North	East	South
---	---	P	1N.T.
P	2N.T.		

Opening Lead: ♥9

This time you are trying to get R.H.O. to make a friendly play. In a previous hand you wanted West to discontinue the suit which was opened. This time, what would you like to see East do on that opening lead?
Play the Ace!

Ask Yourself

1. How many winners do you have?
2. Who is the dangerous opponent?
3. If you win the opening lead, what suit must you attack immediately?
4. If you are allowed to proceed, what will your 8 tricks be?
5. What will you do if R.H.O. wins the opening lead and leads a diamond or does so after winning the ♠Ace?

Dummy

- ♠ QJ
- ♥ Q5
- ♦ 9843
- ♣ KJ972

West
- ♠ 963
- ♥ 9842
- ♦ AQ65
- ♣ 106

East
- ♠ A875
- ♥ AJ10
- ♦ J102
- ♣ 843

- ♠ K1042 (you)
- ♥ K763
- ♦ K7
- ♣ AQ5

Answers

1. Given the lead, you have one heart and 5 clubs.
2. East is the dangerous opponent. You wouldn't want a diamond lead through your King.
3. & 4. You must attack spades. Three spade tricks in addition to one heart and 5 clubs will give you 3N.T. However, don't bemoan the fact that it wasn't bid. A good defender sitting East would take the opening lead – having recognized partner's opening lead as 'Top of Nothing' – and switch to the ♦Jack, down one at 3N.T.

Failing the immediate diamond switch, this same good defender would do so upon winning the first spade.

5. You would have to hope that the diamonds are distributed in such a way as to allow the defenders only 3 diamond tricks.

27. Don't Mess Up the Easy Ones

Dummy
♠ AQJ4
♥ 65
♦ KJ983
♣ 73

♠ K85 (you)
♥ K43
♦ A1052
♣ AJ2

E/W Vul.

West	North	East	South
---	1♦	2♥	2N.T.
P	3N.T.		

Opening Lead: ♥Ace

You breath easy when West's ♥Ace hits the table. West then leads the ♥7.

Ask Yourself
1. How many hearts were originally held by West?
2. Which opponent is the dangerous one?
3. What is the point range of East's hand?
4. Could West have any honour(s) in addition to the ♥Ace?
5. How many tricks are available in diamonds?
6. How must you handle the suit?

Dummy

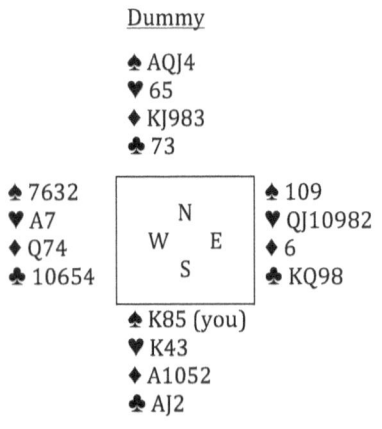

Answers
1. It can only be 2. Your side has 5 of them, leaving 6 for East's weak jump overcall.
2. East's heart suit poses a real danger and East must be kept off the lead.
3. East has between 6 and 11 points.
4. West could only have a Queen in addition to the ♥Ace. Any more would mean that East would not have had sufficient to make the weak jump overcall.
5. There could be as many as 5.
6. You have 8 certain tricks and need one more. After winning trick #1, enter dummy with a spade and lead the ♦Jack, tempting a cover. If it's covered win the Ace and waltz home with 10 tricks. If it isn't covered, let it ride to lose this trick to West. Don't play for the ♦Q to drop. You wouldn't be happy to find 3 to the Queen in East's hand.

28. Which Option is the Best

Dummy
♠ K5
♥ J72
♦ AQ6432
♣ 109

```
      N
  W       E
      S
```

♠ A4 (you)
♥ K109
♦ KJ5
♣ QJ763

You have 8 top tricks. Where you win this first trick depends on which suit you are going to attack in an effort to develop one more.

Neither Vul.

West	North	East	South
---	---	---	1♣
P	1♦	P	1N.T.
P	3♦	P	3N.T.

Opening Lead: ♠Queen

Ask Yourself

1. Could West be leading from 5 card suit?
2. Should you attack clubs or hearts to develop more tricks? Does it matter?
3. If you choose to lead hearts, which card should you be leading?

Dummy

♠ K5
♥ J72
♦ AQ6432
♣ 109

♠ QJ109   ♠ 87632
♥ Q853   ♥ A64
♦ 97   ♦ 108
♣ A84   ♣ K52

```
      N
  W       E
      S
```

♠ A4 (you)
♥ K109
♦ KJ5
♣ QJ763

Answers

1. Since the opponents have 9 spades – likely division being 5/4 – the lead could certainly be from a 5 card suit.

2. In making a decision of this type, project how the play will go if you lead one of them and how it will go if you lead the other one first. As you will discover, it does matter. Leading clubs looks very tempting because you can develop 3 more tricks. However, the defenders have already dislodged one of your spade stoppers. By the time you dislodge their second high club, they will have set up their spades and you'll go down in flames. You should try to make your ♥King. Although a finesse is only a 50% solution, it's better than 0% by trying clubs.

3. Lead the ♥Jack. Most inexperienced players can't resist covering. If it isn't covered, play your King anyway.

29. Lady Luck is Smiling on You

Dummy
♠ 84
♥ J1094
♦ 8632
♣ A92

♠ AKJ10963 (you)
♥ K32
♦ -----
♣ Q103

E/W Vul.

West	North	East	South
---	---	2♦	4♠
Dbl.			

Opening Lead: ♦King

Sometimes you have to simply bid what you think you can make, there being no scientific solution.

Ask Yourself
1. What are your thoughts after trumping trick #1?
2. Where are most of their 22 points?
3. How many diamonds are in West's hand and what are they most likely to be?
4. Where is the ♥Ace?
5. How many losers do you have?
6. What single card could be in East's possession which would enable you to bring in this ambitious contract?
7. With that in mind, how would you play the hand?

Dummy
♠ 84
♥ J1094
♦ 8632
♣ A92

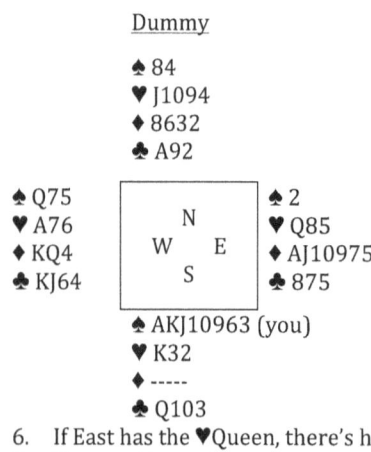

♠ Q75
♥ A76
♦ KQ4
♣ KJ64

♠ 2
♥ Q85
♦ AJ10975
♣ 875

♠ AKJ10963 (you)
♥ K32
♦ -----
♣ Q103

Answers
1. How can I blame this one on partner?
2. East can only have 8 or 9 , having opened a weak two. Most of their points are therefore in West's hand.
3. West has to have 3 diamonds. Leading the King would only have been done with a doubleton. So West must have K/Q/x.
4. The ♥Ace is most likely in West's hand.
5. You have 5. That's why you're looking for a scapegoat.
6. If East has the ♥Queen, there's hope.
7. You need 2 entries to dummy so that hearts can be attacked from that side and eventually be established for a club discard. After trumping the opening lead, give up a trump trick. This creates a second dummy entry. West, not wanting to lead away from the club or heart holdings, will likely exit with a trump. Win dummy's trump 8 and lead the ♥ Jack. You have to hope that East holds the

Queen. If your Jack isn't covered, duck. And if West doesn't take the Ace, lead to the 10. You'll eventually discard a club on dummy's thirteenth heart.

30. An Alterior Motive

♠ A862
♥ 75
♦ 1043
♣ AKQJ

```
    N
 W     E
    S
```

♠ Q10 (you)
♥ AKJ986
♦ 98
♣ 1098

East overtakes the opening lead and returns a diamond to partner's Jack.

Both Vul.

West	North	East	South
-	1♣	P	1♥
P	1♠	P	2♥
P	3♣	P	4♥

Opening Lead: ♦Queen

Ask Yourself

1. Why did East do this?
2. Where is the ♥Queen? Why?
3. How many losers do you have?
4. Where can you get rid of one?
5. What must be your hope?
6. What's your plan?

Dummy
♠ A862
♥ 75
♦ 1043
♣ AKQJ

♠ J75   ♠ K943
♥ Q42   N   ♥ 103
♦ QJ72 W   E ♦ AK65
♣ 653   S   ♣ 742

♠ Q10 (you)
♥ AKJ986
♦ 98
♣ 1098

Answers

1. East did this so as to have a safe exit card on trick #2. This would not be the case if East encouraged partner and won trick #2 instead of #1.
2. It has to be with West. If East had it, in addition to the top 2 diamonds there might have been a bid.
3. You have 4 losers – A spade, one heart and the 2 diamonds already lost.
4. You can discard your spade loser on dummy's ♣Jack.
5. You have to hope that clubs are divided evenly between your opponents.
6. Wind trick #3 and draw two rounds of trump with the Ace & King. If the Queen were to drop, that would be icing on the cake. Now play dummy's clubs and discard a spade. West is welcome to trump the last club with the master trump. You've gotten rid of your spade loser on the same trick.

31. Textbook Stuff

<u>Dummy</u>
♠ AJ103
♥ KJ1072
♦ Q5
♣ KQ

♠ 98742 (you)
♥ Q53
♦ AK86
♣ 4

N/S Vul.

West	North	East	South
3♣	Dbl.	P	3♠
P	4♠		

Opening Lead: ♦Jack

With no intermediates visible, you must conclude that the opening lead is the top of a sequence. You win it in dummy.

Ask Yourself

1. How many losers do you have?
2. Could the King and Queen of trump be seen in the same hand? Which one?
3. Should you begin drawing trump immediately?
4. How can you eliminate one of your losers?

<u>Dummy</u>
♠ AJ103
♥ KJ1072
♦ Q5
♣ KQ

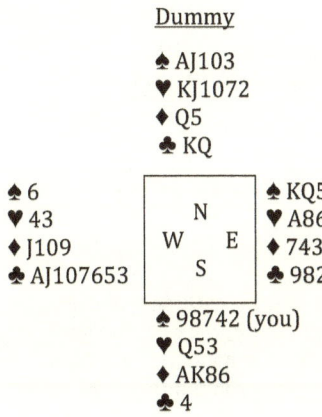

♠ 6   ♠ KQ5
♥ 43   ♥ A86
♦ J109   ♦ 7432
♣ AJ107653   ♣ 982

♠ 98742 (you)
♥ Q53
♦ AK86
♣ 4

Answers

1. You have 4 losers – 2 trump, one heart, and one club.
2. With West having shown 7 clubs, that hand will have some serious shortages. That being the case, the 4 missing trump will likely divide 4/0 or 3/1 with East having more than West. Therefore the King and Queen are very likely with East.
3. When you can't afford to lose the lead, it is unwise to tackle trump. In this case, they would probably lead clubs.
4. You must hope that West's hand has one or zero trump and precisely the J/10/9 of diamonds. Simply cash 3 more diamond tricks, discarding dummy's clubs.

32. D. D. D.

Dummy
♠ QJ
♥ J63
♦ AQ63
♣ J1082

♠ A43 (you)
♥ 1098
♦ KJ75
♣ AK7

N/S Vul.

West	North	East	South
---	---	---	1N.T.
P	3N.T.		

Opening Lead: ♣3

Dummy's Jack wins the first trick. Counting winners, you have one spade, 4 diamonds and 3 clubs.

Ask Yourself
1. Where will you get your ninth trick?
2. What tricks will your opponents get if a spade finesse is unsuccessful?
3. Would a heart lead serve any purpose?

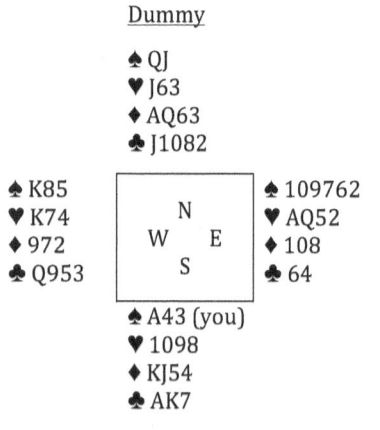

Dummy
♠ QJ
♥ J63
♦ AQ63
♣ J1082

♠ K85   ♠ 109762
♥ K74   ♥ AQ52
♦ 972   ♦ 108
♣ Q953   ♣ 64

♠ A43 (you)
♥ 1098
♦ KJ54
♣ AK7

Answers
1. A successful spade finesse would produce a ninth trick.
2. However, if it loses, the bad guys will get the spade and 4 hearts for down one.
3. Just as bidding a weak minor to dissuade a lead when planning to play 3N.T., leading a weak suit during play accomplishes the same – throwing them off the scent. But it must be done early in the play before your opponents can get a count on the hand. Upon winning the first trick in dummy, lead the ♥3. East will likely duck and West

will win and likely switch to spades – mission accomplished. D.D.D. – Deception demands dispatch. It is worth noting that leading a major – something that such an auction cries out for – would have had more chance for success. It might have been a heart.

33. When all Else Fails, Pay Attention

Dummy
♠ J10
♥ AKQ42
♦ J109
♣ 864

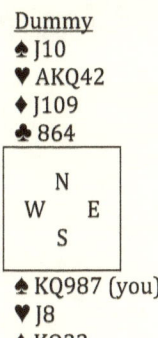

♠ KQ987 (you)
♥ J8
♦ KQ32
♣ 75

N/S Vul.

West	North	East	South
---	---	---	P
P	1♥	2♣	2♠
P	P	3♣	P
P	3♠		

Opening Lead: ♣Queen

East overtakes the opening lead and leads Ace and a small Diamond.

Ask Yourself
1. What is East likely trying to do?
2. Where are the ♣Jack and ♠Ace?
3. How many potential losers do you have?
4. How can you prevent the diamond ruff and also eliminate your 4th loser?

Dummy

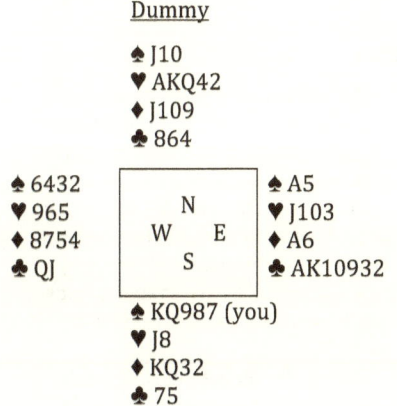

♠ J10
♥ AKQ42
♦ J109
♣ 864

♠ 6432
♥ 965
♦ 8754
♣ QJ

♠ A5
♥ J103
♦ A6
♣ AK10932

♠ KQ987 (you)
♥ J8
♦ KQ32
♣ 75

Answers
1. It certainly looks like East is trying to get a diamond ruff.
2. The opening lead and East's overtake strongly suggest that West has the ♣Jack. East must have the ♠Ace as an entry.
3. You have 4 losers, a spade, a diamond and 2 clubs. And there will be one more with a potential diamond ruff.
4. Take East's ♦6 and lead 3 rounds of hearts, discarding your remaining club. You've served the lines of defence. East, after taking the

Trump Ace cannot get to partner for the diamond ruff. Both your club loser and impending ruff have been eliminated simultaneously.

34. Decisions, Decisions

Dummy
♠ AQ75
♥ J109
♦ AQJ107
♣ 8

♠ 964 (you)
♥ AQ3
♦ K752
♣ KJ9

East plays the 2 on the opening lead and your 9 wins.

E/W Vul.

West	North	East	South
---	1♦	P	2N.T.
3♣	P	P	3N.T.

Opening Lead: ♣7

Ask Yourself

1. Who has the majority, if not all, of their 13 points?
2. How many top tricks do you have?
3. Where can you get one more?
4. Who is the dangerous opponent?
5. How can you get that one more trick without exposing yourself to the loss of all those club tricks?

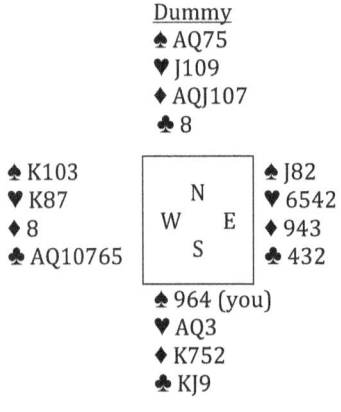

Dummy
♠ AQ75
♥ J109
♦ AQJ107
♣ 8

♠ K103
♥ K87
♦ 8
♣ AQ10765

♠ J82
♥ 6542
♦ 943
♣ 432

♠ 964 (you)
♥ AQ3
♦ K752
♣ KJ9

Answers

1. With West having made a 3 level, vulnerable overcall, it doesn't take a genius to place those missing 13 points.
2. You have 8 top tricks – the club already won, one spade, one heart and 5 diamonds.
3. A successful heart or spade finesse will produce that extra needed trick.
4. East is the dangerous opponent since a club lead from that side would prove to be disastrous.
5. Although it is highly unlikely, East might have the ♠King. Therefore, finessing in spades could be fatal. Take the heart finesse. Even if it loses, as you would expect, your club holding is safe. This also produces a second heart trick, making your total 10 in all.

35. Spot the Technique

Dummy
♠ K10872
♥ AK3
♦ 8
♣ AJ94

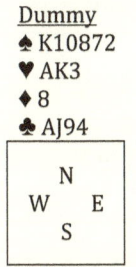

♠ AQJ63 (you)
♥ -----
♦ AK6
♣ 108532

Both Vul.

West	North	East	South
2♦	Dbl.	P	3♠
P	4♣¹	P	4♦²
P	4♥³	P	5♦⁴
P	5♥⁵	P	5♠
P	6♠		

Opening Lead: ♦Queen

1. Four clubs accepts spades as trump and shows first round control of clubs.
2. Four diamonds shows first round control of diamonds.
3. Four hearts shows first round control of hearts.
4. Five diamonds shows second round control of diamonds.
5. Five hearts shows second round control of hearts.

Ask Yourself

1. How many potential losers do you have?
2. Can you trump any losers in dummy?
3. Are there any extra winners, in dummy, on which you could discard losers?
4. Could you establish a suit, in dummy, on which you could discard losers?
5. What declarer play technique could possibly work?

Dummy
♠ K10872
♥ AK3
♦ 8
♣ AJ94

♠ 4   ♠ 95
♥ Q1086   ♥ J97542
♦ QJ10972 ♦ 543
♣ K7   ♣ Q6

♠ AQJ63 (you)
♥ -----
♦ AK6
♣ 108532

Answers

1. You have 2 potential losers – both in clubs.
2. You can trump a diamond in dummy and a heart in your hand but you'll still have those club losers.
3. You could discard 2 club losers on dummy's hearts but you'll still have 2 club losers.
4. There is nothing to establish in dummy.
5. The most logical technique to consider is an 'Elimination Throw-In'. Win the first trick and draw 2

rounds of trump, ending in dummy. You have now eliminated one suit. Cash dummy's high hearts, discarding 2 clubs. Now cash 2 high diamonds and ruff your ♦6. This eliminates a second suit. Now, by ruffing the ♥3 you've eliminated a third suit. Now lead a club and finesse dummy's Jack. East wins but is now faced with a Hobson's choice. A club lead is into dummy's tenace and the lead of another suit gives declarer a ruff and sluff. The elimination of those 3 suits removed East's safe exit cards thus forcing a favourable lead when 'Throw-In' with the club.

36. Being Magnanimous

Dummy
♠ KQ2
♥ AK
♦ AQ5
♣ 98753

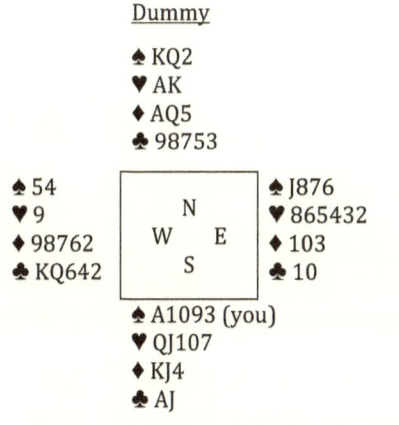

♠ A1093 (you)
♥ QJ107
♦ KJ4
♣ AJ

Neither Vul.

West	North	East	South
---	---	---	1N.T.
P	6N.T.		

Opening Lead: ♦9

The prevailing wisdom when leading against any grand slam or 6N.T. is to be passive. Hence the ♦9, top of nothing.

Ask Yourself

1. How many ironclad tricks do you have?
2. Which is the only suit where you might get one more?
3. How is the suit likely to break?
4. How might you discover who has the critical card in that suit?
5. What is an integral part of gaining this information?

Dummy
♠ KQ2
♥ AK
♦ AQ5
♣ 98753

♠ 54
♥ 9
♦ 98762
♣ KQ642

♠ J876
♥ 865432
♦ 103
♣ 10

♠ A1093 (you)
♥ QJ107
♦ KJ4
♣ AJ

Answers

1. You have 11 certain tricks – 3 spades, 4 hearts, 3 diamonds and one club.
2. Only spades offer the chance of one more trick.
3. Most times when you are missing 6 cards, they will split 4/2.
4. By cashing your winners in other suits you can get a count on the hand. This is known as a discovery play and will reveal which opponent has the four spades.
5. An integral part of discovery is conceding a trick in a suit where you can still maintain control. In this case, it can only be clubs. After winning the first trick, give up a club, win the return and cash your winners in all suits but the critical one – spades. In the process, you'll discover that East started with 6 hearts,

2 diamonds, one club and therefore 4 spades. It is then a simple matter of cashing dummy's high spades and if the Jack doesn't drop, to finesse for it against East. R.T.T. (Retain The Tenace) is good bridge advice and that is precisely what you are doing.

37. A Proven Finesse

<u>Dummy</u>
♠ QJ2
♥ KQ53
♦ 1064
♣ Q32

```
     N
 W       E
     S
```

♠ K75 (you)
♥ A72
♦ Q75
♣ AK109

Neither Vul.

West	North	East	South
---	---	P	1N.T.
P	3N.T.		

Opening Lead: ♠10

East wins the opening lead and switches to the ♦Jack.

Ask Yourself

1. Why has East switched to diamonds instead of continuing spades?
2. Missing the 10, why lead the Jack?
3. How many tricks do you have?
4. Where can you get one more?
5. What do you play on the ♦Jack?
6. How do you continue?

<u>Dummy</u>
♠ QJ2
♥ KQ53
♦ 1064
♣ Q32

♠ 109863
♥ J1064
♦ A2
♣ 75

```
     N
 W       E
     S
```

♠ A4
♥ 98
♦ KJ983
♣ J864

♠ K75 (you)
♥ A72
♦ Q75
♣ AK109

Answers

1. The ♠Ace is East's only entry and diamonds – dummy's weak suit – should be attacked from East's side. Returning partner's suit is not always the best defence.
2. This looks like a 'Dummy Surround' play. East has either the Ace or King. It can't be both or East might have opened.
3. You have 8 – 2 spades, 3 hearts and 3 clubs.
4. An extra trick can come from hearts or clubs if either suit splits 3/3 which is only a 36% chance.

However clubs offer an additional chance via a finesse which is 50/50.

5. If you play your Queen, be ready for a quizzical look or glare from partner.
6. If West doesn't return a diamond after winning the ♦Ace, win it and cash all your winners in the other suits. This will reveal East's distribution as

45

2 – 2 – 5 – 4. Now you can cash a high club, lead to dummy's Queen and take the proven finesse for East's Jack. You could have taken the finesse at any point in the play but since it was of the two-way variety why rely on a guess when following the suggested line made it a certainty.

38. Two Finesses?

Dummy
♠ AKJ53
♥ 86
♦ J42
♣ KJ9

```
      N
  W       E
      S
```

♠ 94 (you)
♥ AQ
♦ AK1095
♣ Q742

Both Vul.

West	North	East	South
---	---	2♥	Dbl.
P	3♠	P	3N.T.

Opening Lead: ♥2

Holding 3 cards in partner's suit but holding no honour and not having supported, standard practice is to lead low. You take the King with your Ace.

Ask Yourself

1. How many tricks do you have?
2. Where might you find the additional tricks needed?
3. Is there danger associated with either line?
4. Who is most likely to hold the ♣Ace?
5. Where might the missing Queens reside?
6. What is the proper technique when faced with two finesses, needing one for success?
7. What now, my Lord?

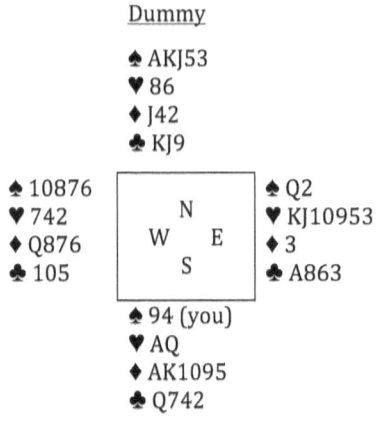

Dummy

♠ AKJ53
♥ 86
♦ J42
♣ KJ9

♠ 10876   ♠ Q2
♥ 742   ♥ KJ10953
♦ Q876   ♦ 3
♣ 105   ♣ A863

♠ 94 (you)
♥ AQ
♦ AK1095
♣ Q742

Answers

1. You only have 6 – 2 spades, 2 hearts and 2 diamonds.
2. A successful finesse in spades or diamonds will produce the extra tricks.
3. Yes, there is danger in finessing. If a finesse loses, your second heart stopper will be dislodged and you'll still be a trick short. When the second finesse loses, too bad, so sad.
4. It most likely is in East's hand.
5. If East had both Queens, the hand would be too strong to open a weak 2. With your luck, if East had one of them, it would be the wrong one.
6. With two finesses for a Queen, try to drop the one where you have the most cards. You have 8 diamonds and 7 spades. If the ♦Queen doesn't fall you can try the spades.
7. However, with the ♣Ace likely with East, why not lead a club from dummy. If the Ace isn't played, you've stolen a trick and can now switch your attention to diamonds. Cash the Ace / King and lead a third round. Now you'll have overtricks.

39. Loser on Loser

<u>Dummy</u>
♠ A753
♥ AK64
♦ 982
♣ 74

♠ K10986 (you)
♥ J73
♦ KJ
♣ AQ5

N/S Vul.

West	North	East	South
---	P	P	1♠
2♦	3♦	P	4♠

Opening Lead: ♥10

The opening lead is likely from Q109, 1098, 10x or could be a singleton. Any of these, other than the singleton, are not especially good leads. This suggests that any other choice would have been worse.

Ask Yourself

1. Where are the ♦Ace, ♦Queen and ♣King?
2. How many losers do you have?
3. What must you hope for in the trump suit?
4. What about hearts?
5. How many diamonds are probably in West's hand?
6. What is your best guess as to the distribution of West's hand?
7. Now what?

<u>Dummy</u>

♠ A753
♥ AK64
♦ 982
♣ 74

♠ QJ
♥ 102
♦ AQ10543
♣ KJ3

♠ 42
♥ Q985
♦ 76
♣ 109862

♠ K10986 (you)
♥ J73
♦ KJ
♣ AQ5

Answers

1. West must have all 3 of these cards to justify a 2♦ overcall.
2. You could have as many as 5 losers.
3. You must hope that trump split 2/2.
4. You must hope for a doubleton heart in West's hand.
5. There are likely 6 diamonds with West.
6. Putting all clues and assumptions together suggests that West's hand is 2 – 2 – 6 – 3.
7. Win the opening lead, cash another heart and draw two rounds of trump. Now, lead a diamond. West wins, cashes a second diamond and

leads a third round. On this third diamond, discard your remaining heart, a loser-on-loser play. West is now endplayed and can either give you a ruff and sluff or lead up to your club tenace. Either way you are able to eliminate the second of your original 5 losers.

49

40. Don't be Frightened

Dummy
♠ AK109
♥ J8642
♦ AQJ
♣ 10

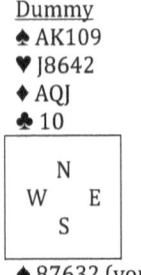

♠ 87632 (you)
♥ Q
♦ 43
♣ K9853

Your partner is certainly from the school of thought which says it's a bidder's game. No matter, the plays the thing.

E/W Vul.

West	North	East	South
2N.T.	Dbl.	P	3♠
P	4♠		

Opening Lead: ♥Ace

Ask Yourself
1. How many points in West's hand?
2. How many losers do you have?
3. How many can be eliminated?
4. After trumping the second heart, how do you proceed?

Dummy
♠ AK109
♥ J8642
♦ AQJ
♣ 10

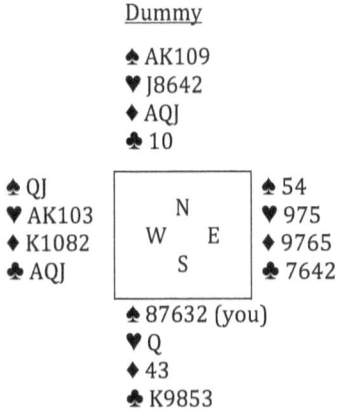

♠ QJ
♥ AK103
♦ K1082
♣ AQJ

♠ 54
♥ 975
♦ 9765
♣ 7642

♠ 87632 (you)
♥ Q
♦ 43
♣ K9853

Answers
1. Since you and partner have 20 and a 2N.T. opener requires 20 or 21, West has all the outstanding points – 20.
2. You have 4 losers, one in each suit.
3. You can eliminate one of the losers by taking the proven finesse in diamonds. Since you knew the location of the missing spade honours, you could have succeeded with two finesses – no matter, they fell.
4. After trumping the second heart, finesse the spade. Trump another

heart and take the second spade finesse, clearing the suit. At this point, you've lost just the opening heart. Because the diamond finesse is certain to succeed, the only other loser will be a club. You can discard two clubs on a good heart and diamond in dummy and trump the other two in dummy. You've made 11 tricks with only 20 points and against a 2N.T. opener. So much for H.C.P.

41. Two Kinds of Finesses

Dummy
- ♠ K3
- ♥ 1072
- ♦ AQJ10
- ♣ K863

```
        N
    W       E
        S
```

- ♠ Q108642 (you)
- ♥ QJ5
- ♦ 7
- ♣ A109

N/S Vul.

West	North	East	South
1N.T.	P	P	2♠
P	3♦	P	3♠
P	4♠		

Opening Lead: ♥Ace

After cashing 2 top hearts and getting no encouragement from partner, West shifts to the ♦9.

Ask Yourself

1. Where's the ♦King?
2. How many points does West have?
3. How many losers do you have?
4. How must you hope that trump are distributed?
5. What must you play from dummy on the ♦9?
6. How should you play the spades?
7. How should the play go for the next few tricks?

Dummy
- ♠ K3
- ♥ 1072
- ♦ AQJ10
- ♣ K863

West
- ♠ AJ
- ♥ AK63
- ♦ 9642
- ♣ QJ5

```
        N
    W       E
        S
```

East
- ♠ 975
- ♥ 984
- ♦ K853
- ♣ 742

- ♠ Q108642 (you)
- ♥ QJ5
- ♦ 7
- ♣ A109

Answers

1. The lead of the ♦9 is most certainly top of nothing. Therefore East has the ♦King.
2. You and dummy have 22 and East has the ♦King. West opened 1N.T. and must have the remaining 15.
3. You have 4 losers – one spade, 2 hearts and one club.
4. You hope that West's spade holding of the ♠A/J is a doubleton. If it is A/J/9, you have 2 spade losers.
5. Play the Ace. You know where the King is and can utilize a ruffing finesse.

51

6. &7. After winning the ♦Ace, play the Queen. If it isn't covered pitch a club. Now lead a club to your Ace and a small trump towards dummy. If the ♦Queen is covered, trump it and then go after trump. You'll be able to discard your losing club later on dummy's established ♦Jack. If you make the mistake of finessing, as many would, when the ♦9 is led, it would be your 3rd loser with the trump Ace yet to come. Too many players fail to make use of the ruffing finesse.

42. Counting, the Nemisis of Many

Dummy
♠ K96
♥ AQ3
♦ 9762
♣ J86

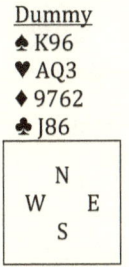

♠ 752 (you)
♥ K62
♦ AKQJ
♣ A92

Not knowing how many clubs you hold
and not wanting to establish dummy's
♣Jack as a trick, West abandons clubs
when you allow the opening lead to hold.
West now leads a heart.

N/S Vul.

West	North	East	South
1♣	P	P	1N.T.
P	3N.T.		

Opening Lead: ♣King

Ask Yourself
1. Where are all defenders' points?
2. How many winners do you have?
3. Where will you get one more?
4. After winning trick #2, what's your plan?

Dummy
♠ K96
♥ AQ3
♦ 9762
♣ J86

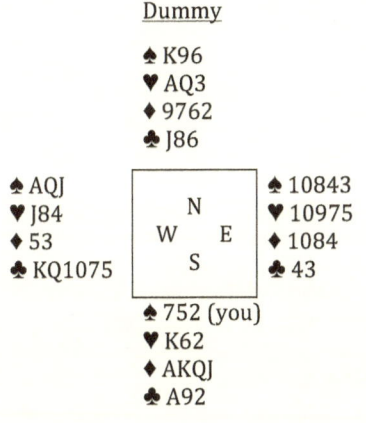

♠ AQJ
♥ J84
♦ 53
♣ KQ1075

♠ 10843
♥ 10975
♦ 1084
♣ 43

♠ 752 (you)
♥ K62
♦ AKQJ
♣ A92

Answers
1. With West having opened the
   bidding, all the missing H.C.P. must
   be there.
2. You have 8 top tricks – 3 hearts, 4
   diamonds and one club.
3. Since both red suits are mirrored,
   neither can provide an extra trick.
   And although you know the location
   of the ♣Queen that knowledge is of
   no use to you. Therefore your only
   hope is to lead towards the ♠King.
4. Win the opening lead and
   immediately lead a low spade
   towards dummy. If West's opening
   bid was to be taken at face value,

you'll have your ninth trick.
An alternative line of play is to take the opening lead and lead a club towards
dummy's Jack.

43. T.M.I. Again

Dummy
♠ 73
♥ 9753
♦ Q42
♣ AQJ7

♠ A6 (you)
♥ AKQ862
♦ J105
♣ 43

Neither Vul.

West	North	East	South
P	P	P	1♥
1♠	2♥	2♠	3♥
3♠	4♥		

Opening Lead: ♠Queen

The opening lead denies possession of the ♠King. And because the opening lead was not a diamond, with defenders holding both the Ace and King, they must be split or both with East. You take the opening lead and draw 2 rounds of trump.

Ask Yourself

1. Could those missing top diamonds actually be in East's hand?
2. How many spades in West's hand?
3. How many losers do you have?
4. How can you eliminate one of them?
5. Of the 3 missing Kings and one missing Ace, how many could East have?
6. What now?

Dummy
♠ 73
♥ 9753
♦ Q42
♣ AQJ7

♠ QJ1052   ♠ K984
♥ J10   ♥ 4
♦ A73   ♦ K986
♣ K108   ♣ 9562

♠ A6 (you)
♥ AKQ862
♦ J105
♣ 43

Answers

1. The top diamonds couldn't be in East's hand because, missing the ♠King, West would need one of them to justify an overcall.
2. West has at least 5 spades.
3. You have 4 losers – a spade, 2 diamonds and a club.
4. A successful club finesse would eliminate one of your losers. A second would allow the discard of your spade loser.
5. & 6. We already know that East has the ♠King and one of the high

diamonds. West most certainly has the ♣King. Finesse it twice to secure your contract.

44. Expert play? Not!

<u>Dummy</u>
♠ KQJ3
♥ 83
♦ KJ5
♣ Q1098

♠ A1098 (you)
♥ 54
♦ 10982
♣ K65

E/W Vul.

West	North	East	South
1♥	Dbl.	2♥	2♠
3♥	3♠		

Opening Lead: ♥Queen

East plays the encouraging 6 on the opening lead. West continues with a low heart to East's King who then exits with a trump.

Ask Yourself
1. How many points do opponents have?
2. How many of those are with East? West?
3. How many losers do you have?
4. What's your plan after winning East's trump exit?

<u>Dummy</u>
♠ KQJ3
♥ 83
♦ KJ5
♣ Q1098

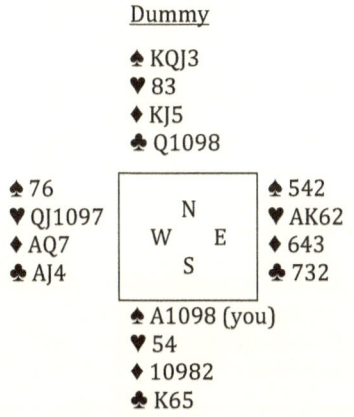

♠ 76   ♠ 542
♥ QJ1097   ♥ AK62
♦ AQ7   ♦ 643
♣ AJ4   ♣ 732

♠ A1098 (you)
♥ 54
♦ 10982
♣ K65

Answers
1. Your opponents have a total of 21 points.
2. Since West opened and East has shown up with the Ace and King of hearts, West must have the remaining 14.
3. You have 5 losers – 2 hearts, 2 diamonds and a club. However, if you handle the clubs poorly there will be an additional one there.
4. You know that West has the A/Q of diamonds and A/J of clubs. Simply win the trump return in your hand and lead a minor suit towards

dummy. If West doesn't play an Ace cover whatever is played. Then return to your hand via a trump, draw the last trump and again lead a minor towards dummy. Following this line, your only losers will be the 2 hearts already lost and two minor suit Aces.

45. Placing Cards

Dummy
♠ AJ5
♥ 109
♦ KJ72
♣ A104

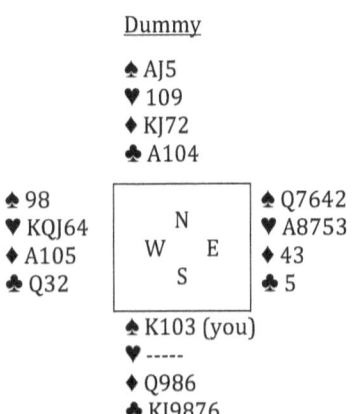

♠ K103 (you)
♥ -----
♦ Q986
♣ KJ9876

N/S Vul.

West	North	East	South
1♥	Dbl.	1♠	2♣
P	3♣	4♥	5♣

Opening Lead: ♥King

You trump the opening lead and take stock.

Ask Yourself
1. Where is the heart Ace?
2. How many points do opponents have?
3. How many of those are with East?
4. Who has the ♠Queen? The ♣Queen?
5. How many losers do you have?
6. You can eliminate 2 of them. How?

Dummy
♠ AJ5
♥ 109
♦ KJ72
♣ A104

♠ 98   ♠ Q7642
♥ KQJ64   ♥ A8753
♦ A105   ♦ 43
♣ Q32   ♣ 5

♠ K103 (you)
♥ -----
♦ Q986
♣ KJ9876

Answers
1. If West had it, it would have been led.
2. They have 18 points.
3. It can't be more than 6. It's hard to imagine West opening with less than 12.
4. It's also hard to imagine East bidding with a suit headed by the 9. The ♠Queen must be with East. Therefore, the ♣Queen has to be in West's hand.
5. You have 3 losers – a spade, a diamond and a club.
6. With proven finesses against the 2 black Queens, you can collect 12 tricks. Fits and helpful distribution take tricks, not H.C.P. Take note bean counters.

46. Two Choices

Dummy
♠ AQ54
♥ AQ2
♦ KJ109
♣ 93

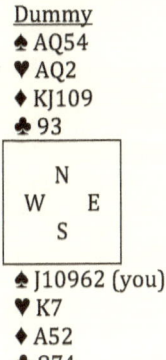

♠ J10962 (you)
♥ K7
♦ A52
♣ 874

E/W Vul.

West	North	East	South
---	---	1♣	P
P	Dbl.	P	2♠
P	4♠		

Opening Lead: ♣Ace

Your opponents take the first 2 tricks with the Ace and 10 of clubs. Not wanting to lead into dummy's tenaces, East leads a third round of clubs.

Ask Yourself
1. How many points do the defenders have?
2. Does West have anything of value other than the ♣Ace?
3. How many losers do you have?
4. Which is the only suit where you might eliminate one of them?
5. How should the play proceed after you trump the third club in dummy?

Dummy
♠ AQ54
♥ AQ2
♦ KJ109
♣ 93

♠ 87   ♠ K3
♥ 9543   ♥ J1086
♦ 7643   ♦ Q8
♣ A52   ♣ KQJ106

♠ J10962 (you)
♥ K7
♦ A52
♣ 874

Answers
1. They have 16 points.
2. If West had anything of value beyond the ♣Ace, East wouldn't have been able to open.
3. You have 4 losers – the 2 clubs already lost, a diamond and a trump.
4. You know where the ♦Queen resides. You can either finesse against it or discard a diamond on dummy's extra heart winner.
5. After trumping that third club, cross to your hand with a heart and try the spade finesse. You know it is

destined to fail. However, there is no damaging play which defenders can make upon winning the spade. And who knows, it may be your lucky day. Win any return, finish drawing trump and cash dummy's hearts, discarding your diamond loser. An alternative line of play, after trumping the club, would be to cash the trump Ace and concede a trump. Either way your losers will be 2 clubs and a trump.

47. Waiting to Make the Opening Lead

Dummy
♠ AJ73
♥ 42
♦ K864
♣ KJ3

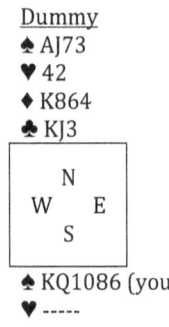

♠ KQ1086 (you)
♥ -----
♦ J102
♣ Q10862

Your first thought after winning the opening lead is to be thankful that your opponents never found their heart fit. Although they couldn't do better than a part score in hearts, some bidding on their part might have kept you out of a very makeable game.

E/W Vul.

West	North	East	South
---	1♦	P	1♠
P	2♠	P	3♠
P	4♠		

Opening Lead: ♠2

Ask Yourself

There really isn't anything to be asking yourself other than why weren't they bidding with a combined total of 20 points. With 11 hearts between them, surely one of them could have bid. It's a bidder's game.

Dummy
♠ AJ73
♥ 42
♦ K864
♣ KJ3

♠ 52   ♠ 94
♥ KJ963   ♥ AQ10872
♦ A95   N   ♦ Q73
♣ A74 W   E ♣ 95
         S

♠ KQ1086 (you)
♥ -----
♦ J102
♣ Q10862

Answers

With proper play by both sides, 4 hearts will be down one, losing 2 spades, a diamond and a club.

Proper play by South will bring in eleven tricks in a spade contract. However, it's the bidding or lack thereof, by E/W which is inexcusable. If opening, East would certainly open with a weak 2 hearts, so why not make a jump overcall of 2 hearts when North opens one diamond. And 2 hearts by West after South's one spade is reasonable. There is no guarantee, but waiting to make the opening lead is tantamount to surrender. Perhaps the vulnerability scared them.

48. Get in There

Dummy

♠ J1085
♥ K83
♦ 873
♣ QJ7

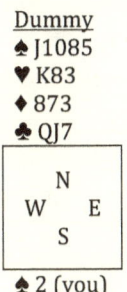

♠ 2 (you)
♥ AJ10942
♦ AK5
♣ 643

E/W Vul.

West	North	East	South
1♠	P	1N.T.	2♥
2♠	3♥		

Opening Lead: ♦Jack

You win the opening lead and survey what looks like a none too rosey landscape.

Ask Yourself

1. How many losers do you have?
2. Where is the ♦Queen?
3. What do you know about the A/K in each of the black suits.
4. How do you plan to win 9 tricks.

Dummy

♠ J1085
♥ K83
♦ 873
♣ QJ7

♠ AQ9743   ♠ K6
♥ Q65   ♥ 7
♦ J109   ♦ Q642
♣ A   ♣ K109852

♠ 2 (you)
♥ AJ10942
♦ AK5
♣ 643

Answers

1. You have 5 losers – a spade, a heart, a diamond and 2 clubs.
2. The opening lead of the ♦Jack denies possession of the Queen.
3. Both black A/K combinations are either split or with East. If West had either A/K the Ace of that suit would have been the opening lead. The opening bid suggests that West has the Aces and East the Kings.
4. You can't trump any losers in dummy, you have no extra winners and establishing a suit for discards is not an option. You must fall back on one of those ever – present options, the finesse. And the only suit offering this alternative is trump. You have no guarantee that West's opening bid contains the trump Queen but logic does suggest it. Take the trump Ace and lead the Jack, letting it run if it isn't covered.

49. "Elementary, My Dear Watson."

<u>Dummy</u>
♠ J1083
♥ AJ10
♦ QJ5
♣ J64

♠ 7 (you)
♥ K97532
♦ K84
♣ AK10

The opening lead of the ♠King means that you know who has the Queen and Ace. "Elementary, my dear Watson". You trump the second spade. Now what?

Neither Vul.

West	North	East	South
---	---	---	1♥
1♠	3♥	P	4♥

Opening Lead: ♠King

Ask Yourself
1. Where are they?
2. How many points do the defenders have?
3. How many of those are in West's hand?
4. How many losers do you have?
5. What's your line of play?

<u>Dummy</u>
♠ J1083
♥ AJ10
♦ QJ5
♣ J64

♠ KQ542
♥ Q86
♦ A10
♣ Q92

♠ A96
♥ 4
♦ 97632
♣ 8753

♠ 7 (you)
♥ K97532
♦ K84
♣ AK10

Answers
1. The King promises the Queen, so West has it and East the Ace.
2. They have 17 points.
3. West made the overcall so the majority of those 17 points are with West. It wouldn't be unreasonable to conclude that the ♠Ace is East's only honour.
4. You have 4 losers – one in each suit.
5. Just to give yourself an extra edge, after trumping the second spade, lead a small diamond. Whether it's this trick or a subsequent diamond, you'll be in dummy to lead the

♥Jack. Some players can't resist covering an honour. When the Jack isn't covered, go up with your trump King and finesse through West for the Trump Queen. When this succeeds your only losers will be those left in the other 3 suits. This extra edge is known as a 'Tempt-a-cover'. "Elementary, my dear Watson".

50. Finessaholics

<u>Dummy</u>
♠ 7532
♥ A5
♦ AQ10964
♣ 9

♠ AKJ10 (you)
♥ 87
♦ 53
♣ QJ862

N/S Vul.

West	North	East	South
---	1♦	1♥	2♣
2♥	P	P	2♠
3♥	3♠	P	4♠

Opening Lead: ♦7

West leads the diamond instead of their suit. Hmmm?

Ask Yourself
1. Why the diamond lead?
2. What is the most likely distribution of trump?
3. Where will the trump Queen be, most times?
4. Should you take the diamond finesse?
5. Should you take the trump finesse?
6. Now what?

<u>Dummy</u>

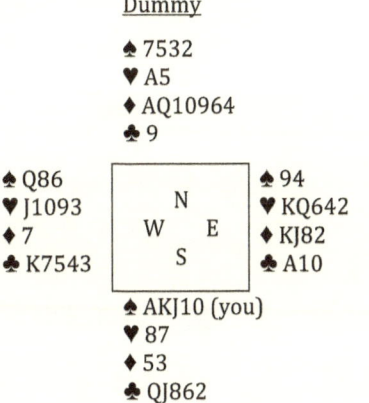

♠ 7532
♥ A5
♦ AQ10964
♣ 9

♠ Q86
♥ J1093
♦ 7
♣ K7543

♠ 94
♥ KQ642
♦ KJ82
♣ A10

♠ AKJ10 (you)
♥ 87
♦ 53
♣ QJ862

Answers
1. You can bet your life that it's a singleton.
2. The trump are likely split 3/2.
3. Since West has a singleton diamond, West's hand likely has 3 spades. That being the case, that's where the Queen will likely be.
4. If suicide is your thing, take it.
5. No. Only finessaholics take low percentage finesses.
6. Take the ♦Ace, two rounds of trump and concede a diamond. You can then trump out the ♦Jack and discard your losing heart on the good diamond. West can trump a diamond but will be trumping with the master card. Your only losers will be the diamond, a trump and a club.

61

QUESTIONS FOR DEFENDERS

Preface

There is an interesting parallel between golf and bridge. Eighteen hole courses normally have 4 par 3s, 4 par 5s, and 10 par 4 holes. Each of these holes has 2 putts allotted to it. That means that half the shots are putts. Yet, we often see the average golfer practicing on a range but seldom on a putting green. It therefore follows that improving your putting will improve your game.

Similarly, in bridge, over the long haul you'll be declarer ¼ of the time and defend ½ of the time. Yet, most bridge players will spend much time learning every convention which comes along. And although improving your bidding will improve your game, it's the knowledge of basics which needs to be improved and not the implementation of many conventions.

As far as the actual play of hands is concerned most players will spend a disproportionate time on declarer play and little on defence. Yet, if you are defending half the time, it stands to reason that improving your defensive play will make you a much better player much more quickly. Vive la defence.

1. Any Port in a Storm

```
            ♠ 32
            ♥ AJ2
            ♦ KQJ104
            ♣ 864
You
♠ 10987     ┌─────────┐
♥ K6        │    N    │
♦ 9752      │  W   E  │
♣ AK2       │    S    │
            └─────────┘
```

Opening bids of 4 normally show an 8 card suit. However in the case of the major suits, there are those who open 4 showing a hand of exactly 5 losers. This is one of those latter openings. You cash the ♣Ace, see partner's discouraging 3, declarer's suspected singleton and look for a switch.

E/W Vul.

West	North	East	South
---	---	---	4♠

Opening Lead: ♣Ace

Ask Yourself
1. What in dummy should concern you?
2. How can you possibly neutralize that suit?

<u>Dummy</u>

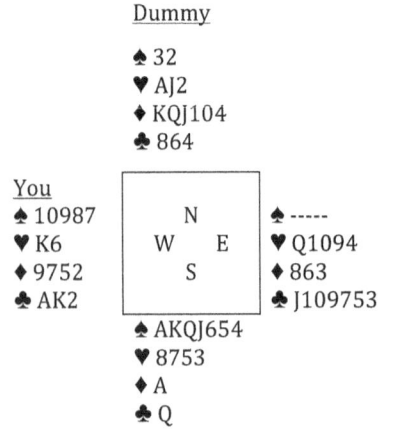

```
            ♠ 32
            ♥ AJ2
            ♦ KQJ104
            ♣ 864
You
♠ 10987     ┌─────────┐ ♠ -----
♥ K6        │    N    │ ♥ Q1094
♦ 9752      │  W   E  │ ♦ 863
♣ AK2       │    S    │ ♣ J109753
            └─────────┘
            ♠ AKQJ654
            ♥ 8753
            ♦ A
            ♣ Q
```

called the 'Merrimac Coup'.

Answers

1. Those diamonds in dummy should sound alarm bells for you. They are a potential 4 tricks for declarer. And if declarer has the Ace, there could be 5 tricks in that suit. However, declarer's bid indicates much shortness elsewhere. Even if declarer has the ♦Ace, it could be alone.
2. If the ♥Ace is declarer's only entry to dummy, get rid of it now. Lead your ♥King to trick #2. If declarer ducks, lead the 6. Sacrificing a high honour to eliminate an entry is

2. The Only Hope

```
            ♠ K73
            ♥ 96
            ♦ 95
            ♣ AQJ1043
You
♠ J96          ┌──────────┐
♥ A8532        │    N     │
♦ QJ10         │  W   E   │
♣ 96           │    S     │
               └──────────┘
```

Although such an auction normally demands a major suit lead, many would choose the ♦Queen, top of a sequence. Partner plays the discouraging 2 as declarer wins with the King. Declarer now leads the ♥Jack.

Neither Vul.

West	North	East	South
---	---	P	1N.T.
P	3N.T.		

Opening Lead: ♦Queen

Ask Yourself

1. Why isn't declarer attacking clubs?
2. Where's the ♦Ace?
3. How many H.C.P. does declarer have? Where?
4. If you win the ♥Jack, what do you play next?

Dummy

```
            ♠ K73
            ♥ 96
            ♦ 95
            ♣ AQJ1043
You                        ┌──────────┐
♠ J96          │    N     │         ♠ AQ105
♥ A8532        │  W   E   │         ♥ 1074
♦ QJ10         │    S     │         ♦ 87642
♣ 96           └──────────┘         ♣ 8
            ♠ 842
            ♥ KQJ
            ♦ AK3
            ♣ K752
```

Answers

1. Declarer must have the ♣King. Otherwise establishing clubs would be the first order or business. With 6 clubs available for the taking and a diamond or two available, declarer is trying to steal a heart before cashing those winners.
2. It has to be with declarer or partner would have taken it and returned them.
3. Declarer has from 15 to 17 H.C.P. – the ♣King, the ♦AK and likely the King and Queen of hearts. Declarer can't have the ♠Ace or the hand would be too strong for a N.T. opener.
4. You have to hope that partner has the Queen and 10 of spades along with Ace. Take the heart and put your ♠Jack on the table. The bridge world will start calling you a genius.

65

3. F. D.

♠ J10753
♥ Q5
♦ KQJ4
♣ 82

You
♠ AKQ98
♥ K7
♦ 83
♣ QJ74

N	
W	E
S	

E/W Vul.

West	North	East	South
---	---	---	1♥
1♠	1N.T.	P	3♦
P	3♥	P	4♥

Opening Lead: ♠Queen

A second high spade is trumped by declarer as your partner contributes the 4 and 2 in that order, indicating a doubleton. Declarer cashes 2 clubs, ruffs a third with the Queen and takes the heart finesse.

Ask Yourself

1. How many trump does partner have?
2. What is the distribution of the unseen hands?
3. After winning the trump King, what is the only lead which can lead to victory?

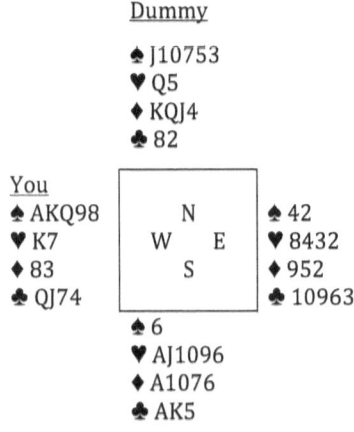

Dummy
♠ J10753
♥ Q5
♦ KQJ4
♣ 82

You
♠ AKQ98
♥ K7
♦ 83
♣ QJ74

N	
W	E
S	

East
♠ 42
♥ 8432
♦ 952
♣ 10963

South
♠ 6
♥ AJ1096
♦ A1076
♣ AK5

Answers

1. Declarer didn't rebid hearts, suggesting only 5, so partner likely has 4.
2. Partner played high/low in the black suits indicating an even number in each. The only logical conclusion is 2 spades and 4 clubs. Although, with declarer having trumped the second spade, you already knew partner had started with 2. Partner's distribution is therefore 2 – 4 – 3- 4 and declarer's 1 – 5 – 4 - 3.
3. After winning the trump King, you

are at the crossroads. This is your only opportunity for success. Lead a third spade. Declarer will ruff, leaving partner with one more trump than declarer. Eventually, partner will trump a diamond and your side will cash 2 clubs for down one. A forcing defence (F.D.) is often best when you have 4 or more trump or you have reason to believe that partner has.

4. 'Mission Impossible'

♠ AK
♥ K9874
♦ 965
♣ Q83

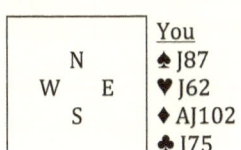

	You
	♠ J87
	♥ J62
	♦ AJ102
	♣ J75

E/W Vul.

West	North	East	South
---	---	---	1♠
P	2♥	P	2♠
P	4♠		

Opening Lead: ♦King

Partner cashes 2 top diamonds and leads a third to you. Believe it or not, you are at the crossroads. There is only one card which you can return to defeat declarer.

Ask Yourself

1. How many points does declarer have? In what suits are they?
2. Could partner have any more points that the 5 in diamonds which you've already seen?
3. What's that magic card?

Dummy

♠ AK
♥ K9874
♦ 965
♣ Q83

			You
♠ 104		N	♠ J87
♥ 1053	W	E	♥ J62
♦ KQ3		S	♦ AJ102
♣ K9642			♣ J75

♠ Q96532
♥ AQ
♦ 874
♣ A10

Answers

1. You and dummy have 20. Partner has already shown 5 in diamonds but could have 2 or 3 more. This leaves declarer with a minimum opening of 12 to 14. Those points can only be in spades, hearts and clubs.
2. Yes. Partner could have any one of the following but only one –
♠Queen, ♥Queen or ♣King. Declarer needs 2 of them to open.
3. The magic card is the 13th diamond. If declarer has a club loser, it can be discarded by establishing the

hearts. When declarer has no more losers, giving a ruff and sluff can do no harm as declarer is discarding a winner. If partner can make an uppercut on the diamond lead, your trump Jack becomes the setting trick. As George Peppard used to say on 'Mission Impossible', "Don't you just love it when a plan comes together?" When the defence has taken all the tricks they can, a trump promotion is often the only winning play.

5. Playing by Clichés

```
            ♠ AK987
            ♥ KJ5
            ♦ 642
            ♣ Q4
You
♠ QJ102      ┌─────────┐
♥ 863        │    N    │
♦ 98         │  W   E  │
♣ AK109      │    S    │
             └─────────┘
```

N/S Vul.

West	North	East	South
---	1♠	P	2♥
P	3♥	P	4♦
P	4♥		

Opening Lead: ♣Ace

Declarer trumps your second club and leads a heart. Partner wins and leads a second heart. Declarer wins and draws your last trump. Declarer has started with 5 hearts, one club and a diamond control. Declarer now cashes 3 top diamonds.

Ask Yourself
1. If declarer's next lead is a spade, should you cover?
2. If you do, how will declarer proceed?
3. If you don't, what is declarer likely to do?

```
Dummy
            ♠ AK987
            ♥ KJ5
            ♦ 642
            ♣ Q4
You                          ♠ 3
♠ QJ102      ┌─────────┐     ♥ A4
♥ 863        │    N    │     ♦ J1075
♦ 98         │  W   E  │     ♣ J87652
♣ AK109      │    S    │
             └─────────┘
            ♠ 654
            ♥ Q10972
            ♦ AKQ3
            ♣ 3
```

Answers
1. Whether or not you cover depends on how many spades declarer has?
2. If declarer has 3 and you cover, declarer will win, concede a spade to you and finesse against your remaining honour. If declarer has only 2, you should duck.
3. You can be reasonably certain that declarer will play high if you don't cover. How would you know? Simple, the diamonds snitched on declarer. When declarer cashed the diamonds, partner first played the 7 and then the 5, indicating an even number of diamonds, which could only be 4. This revealed declarer's distribution to be 3 – 5 – 4 – 1. This will leave declarer with a loser in each suit. So much for the cliché of splitting your honours.

68

6. Some Hope is Better Than No Hope

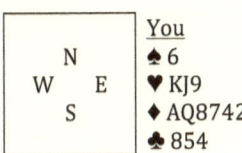

♠ 875
♥ 10642
♦ 93
♣ A1093

		You
	N	♠ 6
W	E	♥ KJ9
	S	♦ AQ8742
		♣ 854

E/W Vul.

West	North	East	South
1♦	P	3♦	3♠

Opening Lead: ♦6

You win the first trick with your Ace and pause to consider the defence. Partner's lead suggests that declarer had a singleton. And if partner has a club honour, it is finessable.

Ask Yourself
1. What is the only suit which offers any chance of success?
2. Which card in that suit might declarer have which would make your choice of card critical?
3. If all is as you envision, which card must you lead to trick #2?

Dummy

♠ 875
♥ 10642
♦ 93
♣ A1093

♠ Q103			You
♥ A83	N		♠ 6
♦ KJ106	W	E	♥ KJ9
♣ K62	S		♦ AQ8742
			♣ 854

♠ AKJ942
♥ Q75
♦ 5
♣ QJ7

Answers
1. It can only be hearts. Here are two clichés which have some merit. "Lead up to weakness" and this poem.
   When the dummy's on your right,
   Lead the weakest suit in sight.
2. You hope it's the Queen. If declarer has both the Ace and Queen your cause is hopeless.
3. You must lead the ♥Jack. Notice that you hold a tenace over dummy's 10. Leading the Jack is called the 'Dummy Surround' play. If you lead any other heart, declarer

can prevail. With your use of another of the game's clichés your tricks will be one spade, 3 hearts and a diamond for down one.

7. Once Again, Your Only Hope

                    ♠ K972
                    ♥ 7
                    ♦ AK7654
                    ♣ AK

On the opening lead, partner's 9 is taken by declarer's Queen. Declarer now leads a low spade.

You
♠ A85
♥ A10843   N
♦ 109   W   E
♣ QJ4   S

E/W Vul.

West	North	East	South
1♥	Dbl.	P	1N.T.
P	3N.T.		

Opening Lead: ♥4

Ask Yourself

1. Why isn't declarer playing diamonds?
2. What must your partner hold in hearts and diamonds to enable defeat of declarer?
3. Should you play your ♠Ace? Why?
4. If partner has the cards you are hoping for, how many tricks do you expect to take?
5. What are they?

                    Dummy
                    ♠ K972
                    ♥ 7
                    ♦ AK7654
                    ♣ AK

You
♠ A85   ♠ J103
♥ A10843   N   ♥ 962
♦ 109   W   E   ♦ QJ8
♣ QJ4   S   ♣ 9752
                    ♠ Q64
                    ♥ KQJ5
                    ♦ 32
                    ♣ 10863

However, it will be partner's fault.

Answers

1. Declarer is probably trying to steal a spade trick before cashing out.
2. If partner has a protected ♦Queen and 3 hearts, the defence will prevail.
3. If partner has those cards, playing your Ace is critical. You must establish your hearts while partner still has that hoped for ♦Queen. Lead the ♥8.
4. & 5. You expect to take 3 hearts, one diamond and one spade. If partner is totally uncooperative and doesn't have those cards, defeating declarer is just a pipe dream.

8. Counting and Projecting

♠ KQ
♥ J43
♦ KQ652
♣ Q109

You
♠ 864
♥ Q95
♦ J109
♣ K852

	N	
W		E
	S	

Partner takes dummy's Queen with the Ace on trick #1 and returns a heart. Declarer ducks and loses to your Queen.

Both Vul.

West	North	East	South
---	1♦	P	1♠
P	1N.T.	P	2♥
P	3♥	P	4♥

Opening Lead: ♦Jack

Ask Yourself
1. How many points does declarer have?
2. How many in partner's hand?
3. What could partner possibly have to enable defeat of the contract?
4. What must you lead to trick #3?

Dummy

♠ KQ
♥ J43
♦ KQ652
♣ Q109

You
♠ 864
♥ Q95
♦ J109
♣ K852

	N	
W		E
	S	

♠ 732
♥ 108
♦ A873
♣ A643

♠ AJ1095
♥ AK762
♦ 4
♣ J7

Answers
1. & 2. You and dummy have 19. Partner already produced the ♦Ace. If that card is partner's only honour, your cause is hopeless.
3. The only hope is that partner also has the ♣Ace.
4. Lead the ♣2. If partner does have the Ace and returns a club to your King, that will be your fourth trick.

71

9. If Only

♠ J85
♥ K43
♦ 7
♣ KQ10965

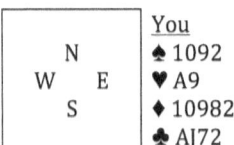

	You
N	♠ 1092
W E	♥ A9
S	♦ 10982
	♣ AJ72

E/W Vul.

West	North	East	South
---	---	---	1♥
P	2♣	P	2N.T.
P	3♥	P	4♥

Opening Lead: ♣4

Partner's opening lead is taken by your Ace as declarer contributes the 8. That lead can only be a singleton or the doubleton 4/3. Of course, fearing a club ruff, declarer might be concealing the 3 to make you think that partner's lead is from a doubleton.

Ask Yourself

1. How many tricks can you count? Where?
2. What must you have to find in partner's hand?
3. How many trump does partner have?
4. What must you lead after winning the first trick?
5. How would the play likely go?

Dummy

♠ J85
♥ K43
♦ 7
♣ KQ10965

♠ K643		You
♥ 876	N	♠ 1092
♦ QJ643	W E	♥ A9
♣ 4	S	♦ 10982
		♣ AJ72

♠ AQ7
♥ QJ1052
♦ AK5
♣ 83

Answers

1. At this point you can see 2 defensive tricks – your Aces.
2. You must hope that partner has the ♠King and a singleton club.
3. Partner must have 3 trump. Declarer didn't rebid hearts, so must only have 5. Dummy has 3 and you have 2, leaving 3 for partner.
4. Lead a spade.
5. It matters not whether declarer wins the Ace or ducks. The dye is cast as long as partner has the King. If declarer does play the Ace and

plays on trump, you take the Ace, give partner a ruff and the ♠King becomes the setting trick. If declarer doesn't play the Ace, partner wins the King with the trump Ace and club ruff subsequently defeating declarer.

10. Declarer Surround

```
          ♠ 54
          ♥ QJ
          ♦ AJ6
          ♣ Q109876

You
♠ QJ10862      ┌─────────┐
♥ 4            │    N    │
♦ Q108         │  W   E  │
♣ K32          │    S    │
               └─────────┘
```

Partner plays the 3 and declarer the 7 on the first trick. Now what?
Question: What might have happened if you overcall 1N.T. with 2 spades? There are those who would.

E/W Vul.

West	North	East	South
---	---	---	1N.T.
P	3N.T.		

Opening Lead: ♠Queen

Ask Yourself
1. Where are the top spades?
2. Does your partner have anything of value?
3. Of how many tricks can you be certain?
4. What suit is the only one to offer even a glimmer of hope?
5. Which card in it should you lead?

Dummy

```
          ♠ 54
          ♥ QJ
          ♦ AJ6
          ♣ Q109876

You
♠ QJ10862      ┌─────────┐   ♠ 93
♥ 4            │    N    │   ♥ 876532
♦ Q108         │  W   E  │   ♦ K753
♣ K32          │    S    │   ♣ A
               └─────────┘
          ♠ AK7
          ♥ AK109
          ♦ 942
          ♣ J54
```

Answers
1. The top spades must be in declarer's hand. Partner's 3 offers no encouragement.
2. Declarer has a minimum of 15 and dummy has 10. You have 8, so partner has 7 at most. Partner could have the ♥King, ♦King or ♣Ace or any 2 but not all 3. If it's the ♥King, dismiss the thought. It can be finessed. And if partner has the ♣Ace, it won't run away.
3. A spade is already in the bag and partner's ♣Ace makes a second.
4. Diamonds offer the only hope of more.
5. If partner had the ♦King, you must lead the 10 to trap dummy's Jack. Your side will now collect a spade, 3 diamonds and 1 or 2 clubs. Imagine using this technique when you have declarer's hidden card surrounded and not a visible one in dummy. You're either clairvoyant, a witch or a peeker.

73

11. Oh Yeah! That's What You Think.

♠ QJ64
♥ QJ103
♦ A875
♣ 6

You
♠ 93
♥ AK9764
♦ 3
♣ A953

Neither Vul.

West	North	East	South
2♦	P	2♥	2♠
P	4♠		

Opening Lead: ♥2

Partner's opening lead can only be a singleton. All honours are visible in dummy and your hand, so it can't be from an honour. If partner had a doubleton, it would have been a higher card.

Ask Yourself

1. How many winners can you see for your side?
2. Which of dummy's side suits looks like a source of tricks for declarer?
3. How do you neutralize dummy's suit?
4. What card, from that suit, do you lead to the second trick?
5. How will play proceed?

Dummy
♠ QJ64
♥ QJ103
♦ A875
♣ 6

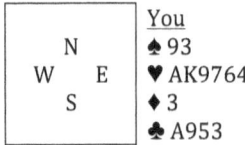

♠ 85
♥ 2
♦ KQJ962
♣ J842

You
♠ 93
♥ AK9764
♦ 3
♣ A953

♠ AK1072
♥ 85
♦ 104
♣ KQ107

Answers

1. You can envision 3 winners – 2 hearts and a club.
2. Hearts will certainly provide a parking place for declarer's losers. With plenty of entries to dummy, a ruffing finesse can be utilized. However, declarer must first draw trump.
3. You can neutralize dummy's hearts by leading them now while partner still has trump.
4. You must lead the ♥4. When giving partner a ruff, the lead of a small card requests the return of the lowest ranking suit (excluding trump and the suit being led). This low heart asks for a club return. Leading a higher heart would have been asking for a diamond (the higher ranking side suit).
5. After winning the ♣Ace, a third heart lead will be ruffed high by declarer but to no avail. However, with your still holding the master heart, you have effectively eliminated dummy's side suit.

12. Thinking Hurts

```
        ♠ Q4
        ♥ K8432
        ♦ QJ104
        ♣ A4
```

You
♠ K95
♥ Q95
♦ 32
♣ 109876

```
        N
      W   E
        S
```

Declarer ducks and partner returns the 5 after winning the first trick. With a successful diamond finesse, declarer cashes 4 diamonds and leads a spade towards dummy.

E/W Vul.

West	North	East	South
---	---	---	1♦
P	1♥	P	1♠
P	3♦	P	3N.T.

Opening Lead: ♣10

Ask Yourself
1. To go along with the Ace, how many more club tricks does declarer have?
2. How many clubs and diamonds will declarer win?
3. Which major suit Ace does declarer have?
4. How many hearts does declarer have?
5. What's your only hope?
6. Once declarer leads the low spade, how should the defence proceed?

Dummy

```
        ♠ Q4
        ♥ K8432
        ♦ QJ104
        ♣ A4
```

You   ♠ 10732
♠ K95   N   ♥ AJ76
♥ Q95   W   E   ♦ K65
♦ 32   S   ♣ K5
♣ 109876
```
        ♠ AJ86
        ♥ 10
        ♦ A987
        ♣ QJ32
```

Answers
1. Partner's play of the King denies the Queen. And from KJ5, the Jack would have been returned. It follows then, that declarer will have 2 more club tricks.
2. Declarer has 7 tricks in the minors.
3. Declarer must have the ♠Ace. If it were the heart, declarer could cash out for 9 tricks.
4. Declarer bid spades after opening a diamond and has already shown up with 4 diamonds and 4 clubs. This leaves room for only one heart.
5. Your only hope lies in heart suit.

6. Take the ♠King and return the ♥Queen. This will result in a spade, a club and 3 hearts for the defence.

13. How Many Do You Have?

♠ A6
♥ J63
♦ 987
♣ KQ1062

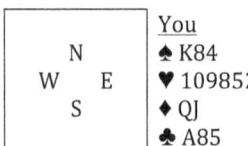

You
♠ K84
♥ 109852
♦ QJ
♣ A85

N/S Vul.

West	North	East	South
---	---	---	1N.T.
P	3N.T.		

Opening Lead: ♠5

Declarer ducks the opening lead, you win your King and return the 8. After winning the ♠Ace. Declarer leads a low club which you duck, partner playing the 3.

Ask Yourself

1. What were you telling partner by returning the ♠8 on trick #2?
2. What was partner telling you with the ♣3?
3. What do you play when declarer leads a second club?
4. Why?

Dummy

♠ A6
♥ J63
♦ 987
♣ KQ1062

♠ Q10953   ♠ K84
♥ Q   You
♦ 10642   ♥ 109852
♣ 743   ♦ QJ
            ♣ A85

♠ J72
♥ AK74
♦ AK53
♣ J9

Answers

1. You are telling partner that you originally held 3 cards. A low card returned would've suggested that you had held 4.
2. Partner is indicating an odd number of cards held. A higher spot would be showing an even number.
3. & 4. Play your Ace. Partner is known to have 3, meaning declarer has no more. If declarer is clairvoyant and knows that the ♥Queen drops, producing an entry to dummy for the established clubs, it is too late because the defenders

will already have the ♣Ace and 4 spade tricks.

Incidentally, the manner in which defenders played their spades and clubs is known as a count signal. Utilizing count signals is an integral part of sound defence. If they aren't part of your defence, they should be.

14. Count Your Tricks

```
        ♠ -----
        ♥ KQ86
        ♦ QJ5
        ♣ KQJ652
```

You cash the A/K of diamonds and discover that partner had a singleton.

```
You
♠ A6
♥ J10753        N
♦ AK843     W       E
♣ 7             S
```

E/W Vul.

West	North	East	South
1♥	P	3♥*	3♠
*Pre-emptive			

Opening Lead: ♦Ace

Ask Yourself

1. How many tricks are you certain of taking?
2. From where can you get any more?
3. What must you lead at trick #3?
4. How will play proceed?

Dummy

```
        ♠ -----
        ♥ KQ86
        ♦ QJ5
        ♣ KQJ652
You
♠ A6                        ♠ 9854
♥ J10753        N           ♥ A942
♦ AK843     W       E       ♦ 10
♣ 7             S           ♣ 10984
        ♠ KQJ10732
        ♥ -----
        ♦ 9762
        ♣ A3
```

ruff will be the setting trick.

Answers

1. You are certain of 4 tricks – the ♠Ace, A/K of diamonds and a diamond ruff.
2. You can get one more trick via a club ruff.
3. You must lead your singleton club.
4. You will lose the club lead. When declarer leads trump, take your Ace and lead the ♦3 for partner to ruff. It shouldn't take partner long to figure out why you lead a club at trick #3. Your ♦3 was your lowest diamond - suit preference signal asking for a club return. Your club

77

15. Return Partner's Suit or Not

♠ J84
♥ 875
♦ KQ10
♣ QJ42

	N		You
W		E	♠ 9632
	S		♥ J109
			♦ 753
			♣ A97

Both Vul.

West	North	East	South
---	---	---	1N.T.
P	2N.T.	P	3N.T.

Opening Lead: ♣10

When dummy is tabled you realize that your only hope lies in the major suits.

Ask Yourself

1. How many points in partner's hand?
2. Which major offers the best chance?
3. What should you lead after winning the first trick?

Dummy

♠ J84
♥ 875
♦ KQ10
♣ QJ42

♠ K7	N	You
♥ AQ63		♠ 9632
♦ J64	W E	♥ J1092
♣ 10987	S	♦ 753
		♣ A5

♠ AQ105
♥ K4
♦ A982
♣ K63

Answers

1. There are 9 pts. in dummy and 5 in your hand. Declarer has announced 15 to 17, so partner must have 9 to 11.
2. Hearts, because of your sequence and dummy's weakness, is the best suit to lead.
3. Lead the ♥Jack. This will bring your side 4 heart tricks. Along with the club already won, that makes 5 for the defence.

16. Heed Partner

♠ Q743
♥ QJ43
♦ 65
♣ Q62

You
♠ AK106
♥ 9
♦ K73
♣ 109853

```
        N
    W       E
        S
```

Partner's 2 on the opening lead discourages a continuation.

Neither Vul.

West	North	East	South
---	---	---	1♥
P	1♠	P	3♥
P	4♥		

Opening Lead: ♠Ace

Ask Yourself

1. You need 3 more tricks. From where will they come?
2. Which of those 2 suits is best?
3. Which card should you lead in that suit?
4. What will be the end result?

Dummy

♠ Q743
♥ QJ43
♦ 65
♣ Q62

You
♠ AK106
♥ 9
♦ K73
♣ 109853

```
        N
    W       E
        S
```

East
♠ J982
♥ 7
♦ A10942
♣ KJ7

♠ 5
♥ AK108652
♦ QJ8
♣ A4

Answers

1. More tricks can only come from the minors.
2. Leading clubs follows a basic guideline of defence – lead through strength.
3. There is only one logical club to lead – the 10, top of sequence.
4. Whatever declarer does, your side will get one club, 2 diamonds and the spade already in. Had you tried to cash a second spade, declarer's losing club would have disappeared on dummy's spade Queen. Heeding partner's advice proves, once again, that bridge is a partnership.

17. Once Again, Let Partner Guide You

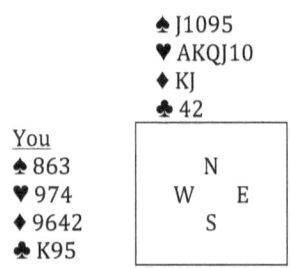

♠ J1095
♥ AKQJ10
♦ KJ
♣ 42

You
♠ 863
♥ 974
♦ 9642
♣ K95

As experienced players will attest, having all the Aces and Kings doesn't guarantee a grand slam. Similarly, having all 4 Aces doesn't produce a small slam. Too often a small slam is undertaken with 2 quick losers in a side suit. However, defenders must play properly to get them.

N/S Vul.

West	North	East	South
---	1♥	P	1♠
P	3♠	P	4♦
P	4♥	P	4N.T.*
P	5♣	Dbl.**	6♠

*1430, **Lead Directing

Opening Lead: ?

Ask Yourself
(Before making the opening lead.)
1. What are the meanings of the 4♦ and 4♥ bids?
2. How many key cards does North have?
3. What is it?
4. Why is partner doubling 5♣?
5. What should your opening lead be?

Dummy

♠ J1095
♥ AKQJ10
♦ KJ
♣ 42

You
♠ 863
♥ 974
♦ 9642
♣ K95

East
♠ 72
♥ 863
♦ 853
♣ AJ876

South
♠ AKQ4
♥ 52
♦ AQ107
♣ Q103

Answers
1. The 4♦ and 4♥ bids show first round control of those respective suits.
2. L.H.O. (North) has only one key card. Playing 1430 a club bid shows 1 or 4 key cards and it's unlikely that R.H.O. (South) was asking for key cards with only one of his own.
3. With North having shown first round control of hearts, need we say more.
4. Doubling an artificial bid – in this case a response to 1430 – asks for a lead of the doubled suit.

5. You should lead the ♣5. Not only is this the norm – 3rd highest from an honour – it also keeps your King poised over an honour which declarer might have.

18. He Who Knows, Goes

♠ KQ87
♥ 86
♦ KJ98
♣ 1043

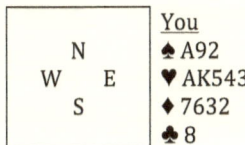

You
♠ A92
♥ AK543
♦ 7632
♣ 8

Neither Vul.

West	North	East	South
---	---	1♥	1♠
4♥	4♠	P	P
5♥	5♠		

Opening Lead: ♥Queen

If partner's opening lead is allowed to win, the defence might not be clear from that side of the table. You know what must be done.

Ask Yourself
1. How many hearts does declarer have?
2. Where are declarer's points?
3. How many tricks do you think you have?
4. Where could additional tricks be?
5. Should you take control?
6. If you do, how should the play go.

Dummy

♠ KQ87
♥ 86
♦ KJ98
♣ 1043

♠ -----
♥ QJ107
♦ 1054
♣ QJ9765

You
♠ A92
♥ AK543
♦ 7632
♣ 8

♠ J106543
♥ 92
♦ AQ
♣ AK2

Answers
1. Declarer cannot have more than 2 hearts. Partner must have at least 4 to have jumped to game.
2. You can see the top 3 spades and your side most certainly has the hearts. Therefore, declarer's points can only be in the minors.
3. & 4. You have 2 Aces and possibly the King. However, if declarer has a singleton heart, the only source for a third trick will be via a club ruff.
5. Absolutely!
6. Overtake partner's opening lead

and lead your singleton club. When declarer leads trump take the Ace and lead a heart to partner's Jack, which was promised by the ♥Queen lead. A club ruff will be your 3rd trick. Can you see how declarer might overcome such a stellar defence?

19. Work It Out

♠ AKJ5
♥ AJ3
♦ 74
♣ AJ109

Declarer wins the ♣Ace in dummy as partner plays the encouraging 8. Declarer now runs the ♦7 which you win with your Jack.

You
♠ 10872
♥ 10952
♦ AJ2
♣ 74

```
      N
  W       E
      S
```

Both Vul.

West	North	East	South
---	1♣	P	1♦
P	2N.T.	P	3♦

Opening Lead: ♣7

Ask Yourself

1. Where are the King and Queen of clubs?
2. How many certain tricks do you have?
3. How many more tricks could there be for you?
4. What should you be leading after winning the ♦Jack?

Dummy

♠ AKJ5
♥ AJ3
♦ 74
♣ AJ109

You
♠ 10872
♥ 10952
♦ AJ2
♣ 74

```
      N
  W       E
      S
```

♠ Q94
♥ KQ6
♦ 65
♣ KQ832

♠ 63
♥ 874
♦ KQ10983
♣ 65

Answers

1. Partner likely has both.
2. You have 2 diamond tricks and one club.
3. Declarer has shown a strong suit but a weak hand. Your side can possibly take 2 hearts.
4. Lead the ♥10, top of touching honours. With this defence you'll get those 2 heart tricks, 2 diamonds and a club for down one.

82

20.   From the Right Side

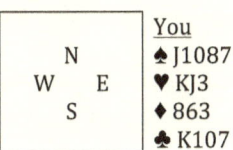

♠ KQ3
♥ A82
♦ 74
♣ AJ432

```
          You
    N     ♠ J1087
 W     E  ♥ KJ3
    S     ♦ 863
          ♣ K107
```

Neither Vul.

West	North	East	South
---	---	---	1♦
P	2♣	P	2N.T.
P	3N.T.		

Opening Lead: ♦2

On the opening lead, declarer takes your 8 with the 9. Declarer now plays the ♥4, partner the ♥9 and dummy the 2.

Ask Yourself

1. Why is declarer ducking partner's ♥9?
2. How many tricks do you have?
3. How many more do you need?
4. Which is the only suit that can provide them?
5. From which side must that suit be led?
6. What heart should you play on that second trick?

Dummy

♠ KQ3
♥ A82
♦ 74
♣ AJ432

```
♠ 42        N      You
♥ 976    W     E   ♠ J1087
♦ AJ102     S      ♥ KJ3
♣ Q865             ♦ 863
                   ♣ K107
         ♠ A965
         ♥ Q1054
         ♦ KQ95
         ♣ 9
```

Answers

1. Declarer doesn't want any suits being led from your side.
2. About the only tricks that you can be certain of are the rounded Kings.
3. You need 3 more.
4. Those extra tricks can only come from clubs.
5. Clubs must be led from your side.
6. Take the second trick with your ♥Jack and lead the ♣7. Partner's Queen will force the Ace and you'll be left with the K/10 over the Jack. Your side will end up with 2 clubs, 2 hearts and the ♦Ace.

21. Tell Partner

♠ 72
♥ QJ3
♦ A10654
♣ KJ4

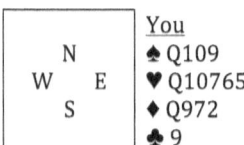

You
♠ Q109
♥ Q10765
♦ Q972
♣ 9

N/S Vul.

West	North	East	South
---	---	---	1N.T.
P	3N.T.		

Opening Lead: ♠6

Declarer takes your ♠Queen with the King. Declarer now leads a low club to dummy's King and leads a small club from dummy.

Ask Yourself

1. Does declarer have any more spade honours?
2. How many H.C.P. does partner have?
3. Could partner have any of these 3 – ♥Ace, ♦King or ♣Queen?
4. What should you discard when dummy leads the small club?

Dummy
♠ 72
♥ QJ3
♦ A10654
♣ KJ4

♠ AJ863   ♠ Q109
♥ 94   N   ♥ Q10765
♦ 83   W   E   ♦ Q972
♣ Q752   S   ♣ 9

You

♠ K54
♥ A82
♦ KJ
♣ A10863

Answers

1. Applying the 'Rule of 11' on the first trick reveals that declarer had only one card higher than the 6, the King played on the first trick. Therefore declarer no longer has a spade honour.
2. If declarer has 15 to 17, partner has from 5 to 7.
3. Declarer must have the ♥Ace and ♦King to make opening 1N.T. feasible. You must hope partner has the ♣Queen otherwise you might as well deal the next hand.

4. Since partner's hoped for ♣Queen would serve as an entry, tell partner that spades will run by discarding the ♠10.

22. Cash Your Tricks

♠ AQ107
♥ 63
♦ K654
♣ 975

	You
N	♠ 852
W E	♥ KQJ72
S	♦ A1098
	♣ 4

Neither Vul.

West	North	East	South
---	---	---	1♣
P	1♠	2♥	3♣
3♥	4♣	4♥	5♣
Dbl.			

Opening Lead: ♥4

You cover partner's opening lead with the Jack and declarer wins the Ace. Declarer now cashes the ♣Ace, hoping to drop the King, and leads a second club. Partner wins and leads the ♦Queen.

Ask Yourself
1. How many hearts does declarer have? Diamonds?
2. Where are you getting 2 more tricks?
3. What should you play on partner's ♦Queen?

Dummy

♠ AQ107
♥ 63
♦ K654
♣ 975

♠ 964	N	You
♥ 10854	W E	♠ 852
♦ QJ32	S	♥ KQJ72
♣ K3		♦ A1098
		♣ 4

♠ KJ3
♥ A9
♦ 7
♣ AQJ10862

Answers
1. Partner showed excellent support in hearts and led the 4. Since the 3 was in dummy and the 2 in your hand, partner's lead is very likely 4th highest. So, declarer has a second heart. If partner also has 4 diamonds, declarer will only have one.
2. They can only come from the ♥King and ♦Ace.
3. You can't be sure that partner won't continue with diamonds when declarer ducks the Queen. Even if declarer doesn't have the missing

spade honours, they are obviously finessable, conceivably providing declarer with a talking spot for a losing heart. You must take your ♦Ace and cash a heart trick. Can you see how declarer could have made the contract?

23. Counting, Again?

♠ 95
♥ Q7
♦ Q8642
♣ AQJ3

	N	
W		E
	S	

You
♠ QJ10632
♥ A95
♦ 10
♣ 1085

E/W Vul.

West	North	East	South
---	---	---	1♦
P	2♦	2♠	3♦
4♠	P	P	5♦

Opening Lead: ♠Ace

Partner leads the ♠Ace. Believe it or not, you are at the crossroads.

Ask Yourself

1. How many spades does declarer have and you need to answer this question before you see the King drop? Diamonds?
2. How are declarer's hearts and clubs likely divided?
3. Which tricks must you hope to take?
4. What must you contribute to the first trick?

Dummy
♠ 95
♥ Q7
♦ Q8642
♣ AQJ3

♠ A874
♥ KJ1063
♦ 7
♣ K64

	N	
W		E
	S	

You
♠ QJ10632
♥ A95
♦ 10
♣ 1085

♠ K
♥ 842
♦ AKJ953
♣ 972

Answers

1. With partner's enthusiastic support, declarer couldn't possibly have more than a singleton spade. And having bid to the 5 level, fewer than 6 diamonds is inconceivable.
2. Declarer has 6 cards, maybe only 5, in hearts and clubs. Those two suits are likely 3/3 or 4/2 in declarer's hand.
3. Any missing clubs would be in partner's hand, making them finessable. You have to hope that you can take 2 heart tricks to go with the ♠Ace.

4. Partner must also be counting and realize that declarer won't have more than a singleton spade. Therefore when you play a high spade on the first trick, partner should be able to read that as a signal for the lead of the higher ranking side suit, hearts.

24. Keep At It

♠ K98762
♥ 5
♦ AQ9
♣ Q104

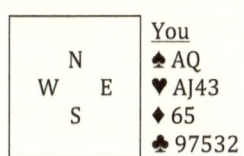

	You
N	♠ AQ
W E	♥ AJ43
S	♦ 65
	♣ 97532

Both Vul.

West	North	East	South
---	---	---	1N.T.
P	4♥	P	4♠

Opening Lead: ♥10

You take partner's opening lead with the Ace. With the A/Q of spades yet to be won, where will you get one more.

Ask Yourself

1. Which is the only suit which offers hope?
2. What must you hope partner has in clubs?
3. How do you project the play?
4. What card do you lead to trick #2?

Dummy

♠ K98762
♥ 5
♦ AQ9
♣ Q104

		You
♠ 543	N	♠ AQ
♥ 1098	W E	♥ AJ43
♦ 10872	S	♦ 65
♣ K6		♣ 97532

♠ J10
♥ KQ76
♦ KJ43
♣ AJ8

Answers

1. Your only hope is in clubs.
2. If declarer opened N.T. with only 15 pts., partner could have the ♣King. You must also hope that partner's King is a doubleton.
3. & 4. Depending on how your partnership handles combinations of spots, you could lead the 9 or 7. Regardless of your methods, partner will realize that you are not interested in a return. Partner's return is really of no consequence, declarer's fate is sealed. When declarer attacks trump, you win and

and lead another club. This eliminates the suit from partner's hand. When you get in with a second trump, you lead a third round of clubs and partner ruffs. As long as partner has a third trump, this defence cannot fail.

25. Leave No Doubt

♠ Q52
♥ 876
♦ AKJ104
♣ 62

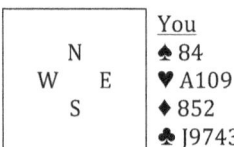

<u>You</u>
♠ 84
♥ A109
♦ 852
♣ J9743

Neither Vul.

West	North	East	South
---	---	---	1♠
P	2♦	P	3♠
P	4♠		

Opening Lead: ♣5

If partner had the A/K or K/Q of clubs, you would have seen the Ace or King as the opening lead. If partner gains the lead again, you certainly don't want another club lead. Play the 3.

Ask Yourself
1. Where's the ♣Ace?
2. What kind of opening hand does declarer have?
3. If partner were to gain the lead, what suit would you want led?
4. Where might partner's entry be?
5. How should play proceed?

<u>Dummy</u>
♠ Q52
♥ 876
♦ AKJ104
♣ 62

♠ K7
♥ KJ32
♦ 963
♣ K1085

```
        N
     W     E
        S
```

<u>You</u>
♠ 84
♥ A109
♦ 852
♣ J9743

♠ AJ10963
♥ Q54
♦ Q7
♣ AQ

Answers
1. Partner would never underlead an Ace. Declarer must have it.
2. Declarer jumped in spades. The hand is better than minimum.
3. You would certainly like a heart lead from partner.
4. & 5. Declarer has the ♣Ace. Partner's ♣King will certainly mot be an entry. Declarer is not likely to lead hearts, so if partner has the ♠King it will be the entry. Declarer will likely cross to dummy with a diamond and try the trump finesse.

When partner wins the trump King, the only logical lead is a low heart. This will get your side 3 heart tricks for down one.

26. The Only Way

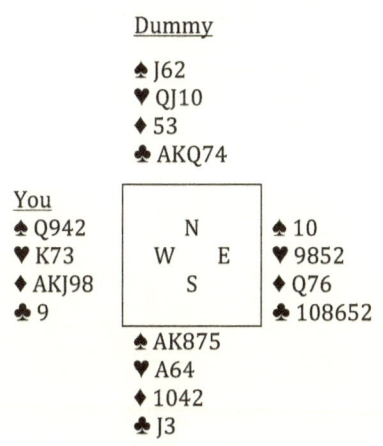

♠ J62
♥ QJ10
♦ 53
♣ AKQ74

You
♠ Q942
♥ K73
♦ AKJ98
♣ 9

```
        N
    W       E
        S
```

E/W Vul.

West	North	East	South
---	1♣	P	1♠
2♦	P	P	2♠
P	4♠		

Opening Lead: ♦Ace

You lead your top 3 diamonds, declarer ruffing the third in dummy. Declarer now leads a small club, wins the Jack and leads a small spade towards dummy.

Ask Yourself

1. What honours does declarer have?
2. Outside of the trump suit what is declarer's only remaining entry?
3. What will happen if you duck the spade lead?
4. What will happen if you take the ♠Queen and return a diamond? A small heart? A trump? The ♥King?

Dummy

♠ J62
♥ QJ10
♦ 53
♣ AKQ74

You
♠ Q942
♥ K73
♦ AKJ98
♣ 9

```
        N
    W       E
        S
```

East
♠ 10
♥ 9852
♦ Q76
♣ 108652

South
♠ AK875
♥ A64
♦ 1042
♣ J3

Answers

1. Declarer got two bids out of a hand where you and dummy have 13 pts. each. Partner has already shown the ♦Queen. It's hard to imagine declarer not having A/K of spades and ♥Ace along with that ♣Jack.
2. It has to be the ♥Ace.
3. If you duck the spade, dummy's Jack will win, two more rounds of trump will be drawn and you'll win only 2 diamonds and a trump.
4. If you take the Queen and return a diamond, declarer will ruff, lead to dummy's ♠Jack, lead to the ♥Ace,

finish drawing trump and claim. If you return a trump, same scenario. In all 3 cases you will win 2 diamonds and a trump. Only by leading the ♥King will you prevail. Once declarer's ♥Ace has been driven out, declarer can lead to dummy's ♠Jack but will have no entry back to finish drawing trump.

27. Obviously

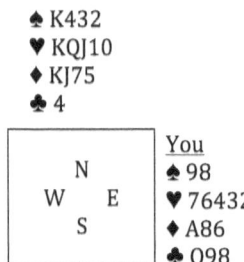

♠ K432
♥ KQJ10
♦ KJ75
♣ 4

You
♠ 98
♥ 76432
♦ A86
♣ Q98

N/S Vul.

West	North	East	South
---	---	---	1♠
P	4♣*	P	4♥**
P	4N.T.⁺	P	5♠⁺⁺

Opening Lead: ♥5

*Splinter Bid – 13 to 16 dummy points, 4 or more trump, and a worthless singleton or void in clubs.
**First Round Control
⁺1430
⁺⁺Two key cards plus the trump Queen.

Partner's opening lead can only be a singleton. Partner wouldn't underlead an Ace and you can see all other honours in dummy. If partner had 985 or a doubleton, a higher card would have been led.

Ask Yourself
1. Is partner looking for a ruff?
2. Does partner have an entry?
3. How will you get on lead to facilitate a ruff?
4. How should the play proceed?

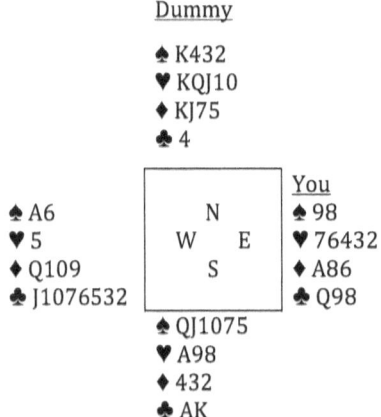

Dummy
♠ K432
♥ KQJ10
♦ KJ75
♣ 4

♠ A6
♥ 5
♦ Q109
♣ J1076532

You
♠ 98
♥ 76432
♦ A86
♣ Q98

♠ QJ1075
♥ A98
♦ 432
♣ AK

Answers

1. Obviously. Why else do players lead a singleton?
2. Having a trump entry is an excellent time to be trying for a ruff. The problem is getting to partner's hand so that you can get that ruff.
3. & 4. On that opening lead you must tell partner where your entry is. Play your highest heart on the opening lead. You can't be asking for a heart continuation, partner has no more hearts. Your ♥7 is a suit preference signal asking for the higher ranking of the two other side suits. When declarer leads trump, partner can win the Ace, lead to your ♦Ace and get a heart ruff – down one. Actually, declarer should have heeded the warning sign during the bidding. When you have excellent values in the splintered suit, this is a serious duplication of values. Declarer should have signed off by bidding 4♠ instead of showing first round control of hearts.

28. Such Extravagance

♠ 63
♥ K1095
♦ 72
♣ AJ1087

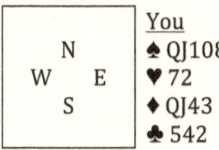

You
♠ QJ108
♥ 72
♦ QJ43
♣ 542

Neither Vul.

West	North	East	South
---	---	---	1♥
1♠	2♥	2♠	4♥

Opening Lead: ♠Ace

When you see the dummy, the needed and precise defence should be crystal–clear. It requires, not only knowledge of the finer signaling points but also precise communication. This combination can be unbeatable and is justly rewarded. Since diamonds should be led from your side, tell partner how to get to your hand.

Ask Yourself
1. How do you do that?
2. When you win trick #2 what card should you lead?
3. What if?

Dummy
♠ 63
♥ K1095
♦ 72
♣ AJ1087

♠ AK954
♥ 86
♦ A1096
♣ 63

N
W   E
S

You
♠ QJ108
♥ 72
♦ QJ43
♣ 542

♠ 72
♥ AQJ43
♦ K85
♣ KQ9

Answers
1. When partner leads an Ace, on the opening lead, in a side suit it promises the King, unless you have made a lead-directing bid. To indicate that you have the Q/J of the suit, play your Queen. You are simply telling partner that, if it is necessary to get to your hand for the switch to another suit, an underlead of the King can be won by your Jack.
2. When you win trick #2 with the ♠Jack, lead your ♦Queen. Your side will then collect 2 diamonds and 2 spades for down one.
3. If you don't adopt this defence, declarer will discard two diamonds on the extra club winners in dummy – after taking trump, that is.

29. Same But Different

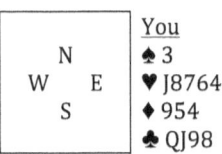

♠ A6
♥ 52
♦ AKQJ62
♣ 753

	You
N	♠ 3
W E	♥ J8764
S	♦ 954
	♣ QJ98

Same introduction as previous hand.

E/W Vul.

West	North	East	South
---	---	---	4♠

Opening Lead: ♣Ace

Ask Yourself
1. What do you play on trick #1?
2. What is partner telling you by leading the ♣10 on trick #2?
3. What suit should you be leading to trick #3? Which card?
4. How should play proceed after partner leads the ♣10?

Dummy

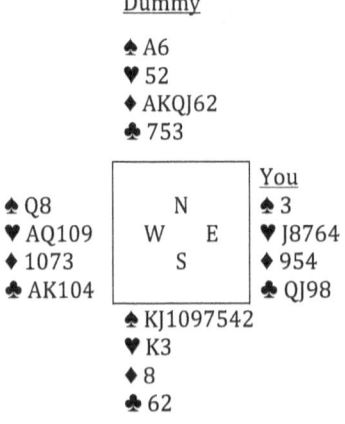

♠ A6
♥ 52
♦ AKQJ62
♣ 753

♠ Q8
♥ AQ109
♦ 1073
♣ AK104

	You
N	♠ 3
W E	♥ J8764
S	♦ 954
	♣ QJ98

♠ KJ1097542
♥ K3
♦ 8
♣ 62

Answers
1. Play the Queen, telling partner that you have the ♠Jack or that the Queen is alone. Either way, if opener needs to get to your hand, you can win the second trick.
2. By leading the ♣10, a suit-preference signal, partner is asking you to return the higher ranking side suit after winning the ♣Jack.
3. As per partner's request, you should be leading a heart – the 6, fourth highest.
4. Partner wins the ♣Jack, returns a heart (a 4th best heart) and you get

you're A/Q for down one. If partner were to lead a trump to trick #2, declarer would collect 12 tricks. If it were the ♣King, declarer would score 10 or 11 tricks depending on whether partner next led the ♥Ace. And if partner were to lead a diamond – ultra passive and inconceivable – declarer would again have 12 tricks.

30. Remember This Play?

♠ 953
♥ A75
♦ QJ109
♣ KJ10

```
        N       You
  W         E   ♠ K1082
        S       ♥ KJ984
                ♦ A43
                ♣ 7
```

N/S Vul.

West	North	East	South
---	---	2♦*	2N.T.
P	3N.T.		

Opening Lead: ♥3

*Flannery – 5 hearts, 4 spades and 11 to 15 pts. Declarer ducks and you win your ♥King. Looking at dummy makes leading spades a logical choice.

Ask Yourself

1. Does partner have anything of value?
2. What might this value be?
3. Which card should you lead in that suit?

Dummy

♠ 953
♥ A75
♦ QJ109
♣ KJ10

```
♠ Q64       N       You
♥ 32    W       E   ♠ K1082
♦ 652       S       ♥ KJ984
♣ 96532             ♦ A43
                    ♣ 7
        ♠ AJ7
        ♥ Q106
        ♦ K87
        ♣ AQ84
```

Answers

1. You have 11 H.C.P. Declarer and dummy have around 26. Partner can't possibly have nay more than 2 or 3.
2. Partner could have any one of the following cards - ♠ Queen and/or ♠Jack, ♥Queen, ♦King or ♣Queen. The ♦King would only produce one trick, the ♣Queen is finessable but on second thought declarer must have the ♥Queen. All of this investigative thought makes a spade lead stand out. For all this

thought to pay dividends, partner must have the ♠Queen. Lead the ♠10, a 'dummy surround' play. Remember the requirements. You must have dummy's card surrounded (you have 10 8 over the 9) and a higher card, here the King. By leading the 10, you hold declarer to one spade trick. Lead any other spade and declarer gets two. More importantly, you get 3 spade tricks to go with one heart and one diamond – down one.

31. Where's The Weakness

♠ QJ9843
♥ K7
♦ Q4
♣ 952

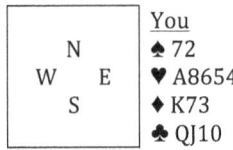

You
♠ 72
♥ A8654
♦ K73
♣ QJ10

E/W Vul.

West	North	East	South
---	---	---	1N.T.
P	4♥*	P	4♠

Opening Lead: ♥Jack

*Texas Transfer.

Dummy plays low on the opening lead. Partner's opening lead denies the Queen. So declarer has it. The normal play is to hold on to your Ace to protect against the King. If you take your Ace, declarer makes both the King and Queen. Over to you.

Ask Yourself
1. What appears to be declarer's weak spot?
2. From which side would it be best to lead that suit?
3. Knowing where the Queen is located, should you be taking your ♥Ace on trick #1?
4. If you take it, what should you lead?

Dummy

♠ QJ9843
♥ K7
♦ Q4
♣ 952

♠ 106 N ♠ 72
♥ J109 W E ♥ A8654
♦ J1052 S ♦ K73
♣ A863   ♣ QJ10

You

♠ AK5
♥ Q32
♦ A986
♣ K74

Answers
1. Declarer's weak spot, looking at dummy, is certainly clubs.
2. Clubs are best led from your hand.
3. You should still take the Ace so that you can lead clubs.
4. Only one card makes any sense. Lead the ♣Queen. With this defence, your side will get 3 clubs and the ♥Ace. Because of your heart play on that first trick, declarer will get to discard one of dummy's diamonds on the ♥Queen. No matter the defence already has the 4 tricks.

32. Don't You Dare

♠ A75
♥ 864
♦ QJ1073
♣ 106

Declarer wins the opening lead and immediately leads a low diamond.

You
♠ 1043
♥ QJ10
♦ AK6
♣ K972

```
        N
    W       E
        S
```

Both Vul.

West	North	East	South
---	---	---	1♣
P	1♦	P	2N.T.
P	3N.T.		

Opening Lead: ♥Queen

Ask Yourself
1. What do you think is declarer's plan?
2. Will partner be of any help?
3. What happens if you take the diamond?
4. What happens if you don't?

Dummy

♠ A75
♥ 864
♦ QJ1073
♣ 106

You
♠ 1043
♥ QJ10
♦ AK6
♣ K972

```
        N
    W       E
        S
```

East
♠ 9862
♥ 9732
♦ 984
♣ Q5

♠ KQJ
♥ AK5
♦ 52
♣ AJ843

Answers
1. Declarer is certainly trying to establish diamonds.
2. Declarer's bidding indicates 18 or 19 pts. You have 13 and dummy has 7. It doesn't take a genius to determine that partner is broke – a King or Queen at most.
3. If you take that first diamond, declarer will win any return, lead another diamond and with the ♠Ace as an entry will eventually prevail.
4. If you don't take it, declarer's plan has been scuttled. Declarer will

lead a second diamond but will be unable to lead a third upon regaining the lead. Getting to dummy with the ♠Ace to lead a third diamond will establish them but declarer will then be unable to get to dummy. The only thing which can upset your applecart is declarer having a third diamond. But in that case, you'll still win the post mortem – at least a small victory.

33. Then What

♠ AK72
♥ 4
♦ AQJ2
♣ QJ109

	You
N	♠ J96
W E	♥ QJ10
S	♦ K985
	♣ 72

Both Vul.

West	North	East	South
---	1♦	P	1♥
P	1♠	P	3♥
P	3N.T.	P	4♥

Opening Lead: ♣Ace

As soon as dummy comes down, good defenders take stock. In the process, they often realize that the normal approach isn't necessarily the best. It's seldom a good idea to play for a ruff at the expense of a natural trump trick. Your play to the first trick has now been determined.

Ask Yourself

1. How many tricks can you see for your side?
2. How will you steer partner in the right direction?
3. Will the correct switch be obvious to partner?
4. How will play proceed if partner follows your lead?

Dummy

♠ AK72
♥ 4
♦ AQJ2
♣ QJ109

♠ Q1084	N	You
♥ 53	W E	♠ J96
♦ 763	S	♥ QJ10
♣ AK85		♦ K985
		♣ 72

♠ 53
♥ AK98762
♦ 104
♣ 63

Answers

1. Three are obvious – 2 clubs and a heart. A fourth will materialize if the defence co-operates.
2. Don't make the normal play of showing a doubleton, by playing the 7, on the opening lead. Partner will cash a second club, give you a ruff and then what.
3. If you play the ♣2 on the opening lead, a switch to diamonds by partner is the only sensible play.
4. If partner does switch, the dye will be cast. Sooner or later you'll get your ♦King for a fourth trick. If

declarer ducks, you win your King, lead a club to partner and sit back waiting for your trump trick. If declarer immediately wins the diamond and begins drawing trump, you win the third round, cash your ♦King and lead to partner's ♣King for your fourth trick. Don't be too quick and play your 7 on the opening lead.

34. Trigger Happy

```
          ♠ 743
          ♥ AJ
          ♦ KQ1098
          ♣ 642
You
♠ K106    ┌─────────┐
♥ Q98653  │    N    │
♦ 653     │  W   E  │
♣ Q       │    S    │
          └─────────┘
```

N/S Vul.

West	North	East	South
---	---	3♣	3♠
P	4♠		

Opening Lead: ♣Queen

Partner overtakes your opening lead, cashes a second club and leads a third. Declarer, not wishing you to trump cheaply, trumps with the Jack.

Ask Yourself

1. You already have 2 tricks, can you see more?
2. How many trump tricks will you get if you overruff declarer?
3. How many if you discard rather than overruffing?

Dummy

```
          ♠ 743
          ♥ AJ
          ♦ KQ1098
          ♣ 642
You                        ♠ 8
♠ K106    ┌─────────┐      ♥ 104
♥ Q98653  │    N    │      ♦ 742
♦ 653     │  W   E  │      ♣ AKJ8753
♣ Q       │    S    │
          └─────────┘
          ♠ AQJ952
          ♥ K72
          ♦ AJ
          ♣ 109
```

Answers

1. You have a third – the trump King.
2. If you overruff declarer, your two remaining trump will fall under declarer's Ace and Queen.
3. If you discard on that third trick when declarer ruffs with the Jack, you'll still have your original trump holding. When declarer tries to draw trump you'll end up with your K/10 sitting over declarer's Queen. This will give you 2 trump tricks, setting the contract.

35. Don't Be Dogmatic

♠ 7432
♥ KJ6
♦ AQ105
♣ 98

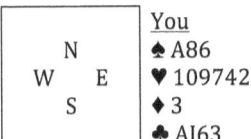

You
♠ A86
♥ 109742
♦ 3
♣ AJ63

Neither Vul.

West	North	East	South
---	---	---	1♠
P	3♠	P	4♠

Opening Lead: ♣King

Partner's lead promises the Queen. What would a dogmatic player contribute to that first trick? And what would a player with a little imagination do?

Ask Yourself
1. How many tricks are reasonably certain for the defence?
2. Can you see any more?
3. To make this vision a reality, what must you do on that first trick?
4. How do you envision the play proceeding?

Dummy

♠ 7432
♥ KJ6
♦ AQ105
♣ 98

♠ 10
♥ 853
♦ K8742
♣ KQ52

You
♠ A86
♥ 109742
♦ 3
♣ AJ63

♠ KQJ95
♥ AQ
♦ J96
♣ 1074

Answers
1. You should be able to take 3 tricks – two clubs and the trump Ace.
2. You might be able to get a diamond ruff but how.
3. You must overtake partner's King on the first trick and lead your singleton diamond. But don't look at partner when you do. You're leading up to a tenace, a no-no. The daggers from partner would be quite painful.
4. However, when declarer goes after trump, you take your Ace and lead to partner's ♣Queen, partner will

become the picture of serenity. It won't take partner long to lead a diamond for you to ruff.

36. Read the Lead

♠ K72
♥ QJ9
♦ AJ10753
♣ 5

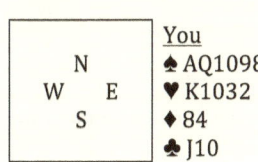

You
♠ AQ1098
♥ K1032
♦ 84
♣ J10

N/S Vul.

West	North	East	South
---	1♦	1♠	2♥
P	3♥	P	4♥

Opening Lead: ♠Jack

Partner leads the Jack of your suit. An honour led, in your suit, on the opening lead can only be from one of three holdings – a singleton, a doubleton or top of touching honours.
Declarer ducks partner's Jack.

Ask Yourself
1. Which is it?
2. You have 2 spade tricks and a guaranteed heart. Where will you get one more?
3. What should you play on that first trick?
4. How will the play proceed if you do?

Dummy

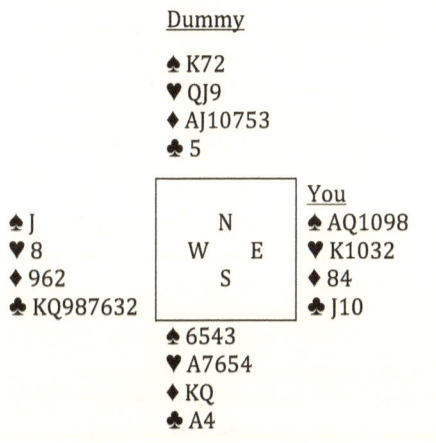

♠ K72
♥ QJ9
♦ AJ10753
♣ 5

♠ J
♥ 8
♦ 962
♣ KQ987632

You
♠ AQ1098
♥ K1032
♦ 84
♣ J10

♠ 6543
♥ A7654
♦ KQ
♣ A4

Answers
1. You have the 10 so it can't be top of touching honours. Partner has one or two spades.
2. A fourth trick can only come from a spade ruff.
3. Overtake partner's Jack with your Queen.
4. Cash your ♠Ace on trick #2 and lead a third spade for partner to ruff. You can then just wait for your trump trick which will be the fourth for the defence. When declarer leads the trump Queen from dummy you can cover it or

wait for the Jack. Either way your trump holding is impregnable.

99

37. Think Ahead

♠ 976
♥ K3
♦ J9753
♣ AK10

```
         You
  N      ♠ KQ852
W   E    ♥ J2
  S      ♦ A86
         ♣ J97
```

Neither Vul.

West	North	East	South
---	1♦	1♠	3N.T.

Opening Lead: ♠10

Partner's opening lead is either a singleton or doubleton.

Ask Yourself

1. Where are the Ace and Jack of spades?
2. How many entries do you have?
3. How many entries do you need?
4. How do you create an additional one?
5. How many entries does partner need?
6. What should you play to the first trick?

Dummy

♠ 976
♥ K3
♦ J9753
♣ AK10

```
♠ 104       N         You
♥ 109874  W   E    ♠ KQ852
♦ K2        S      ♥ J2
♣ 8632             ♦ A86
                   ♣ J97
         ♠ AJ3
         ♥ AQ65
         ♦ Q104
         ♣ Q54
```

Answers

1. Declarer has the Ace and Jack of spades. Partner's lead of the 10 denies the Jack and partner wouldn't underlead the Ace.
2. You have 2 entries – the ♦Ace and a top spade.
3. To establish and then utilize your spades you need 3 entries.
4. You can create an additional entry by ducking the opening lead.
5. Partner needs only one entry – to lead a second spade.
6. Play the ♠8, encouraging partner to lead them again when possible.

Declarer will win the first trick with the Jack and immediately lead diamonds. Partner will win the King and lead another spade. It matters not whether declarer wins this or the next spade lead. When you get in with the ♦Ace you can cash the established spades. The defensive tricks will be those 3 spades and 2 diamonds. Had you not ducked the opening lead, declarer would've had no trouble bringing in 11 tricks.

38.   Where's The Ace?

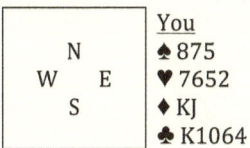

♠ QJ
♥ KQ4
♦ A76432
♣ Q9

```
          You
    N     ♠ 875
 W     E  ♥ 7652
    S     ♦ KJ
          ♣ K1064
```

N/S Vul.

West	North	East	South
---	---	---	1N.T.
P	3N.T.		

Opening Lead: ♣5

Although a major suit lead is normally best, against this type of auction, partner has led a fourth best club. Dummy plays low.

Ask Yourself
1. Where's the ♣Ace? And the Jack?
2. What should you play on that first trick?
3. With how many clubs did partner start?
4. What should you lead to the second trick?

Dummy

♠ QJ
♥ KQ4
♦ A76432
♣ Q9

```
♠ 963       You
♥ 1098   N  ♠ 875
♦ 85  W    E ♥ 7652
♣ A8752  S  ♦ KJ
            ♣ K1064
      ♠ AK1042
      ♥ AJ3
      ♦ Q109
      ♣ J3
```

Answers

1. Partner must have the ♣Ace. You can see the King and Queen of clubs. Why would partner be leading from a Jack high suit instead of beginning with a major. Partner couldn't also have the Jack. Declarer opened 1N.T. You and dummy have 21 H.C.P. Because partner has the ♣Ace, declarer has to have the Jack for a minimum 1N.T. opening of 15.
2. You know declarer has the Jack. Play the King.
3. Declarer played the 3 on the first trick. Partner must have the 2 and therefore started with 5 clubs.
4. You know declarer started with the J/3 of clubs. The 9 and King have gone on the first trick. Lead the ♣10. Partner can take the Ace, felling the Jack and Queen. Partner's 8 – 7 – 2 will then take the last 3 tricks for down one.

101

39. Keep In Touch

♠ J4
♥ 987
♦ KQJ109
♣ K62

```
          You
   N      ♠ Q1075
W     E   ♥ J102
   S      ♦ 6
          ♣ AQ1075
```

Both Vul.

West	North	East	South
---	---	---	1N.T.
P	3N.T.		

Opening Lead: ♣3

As mentioned previously, such an auction cries out for a major suit lead. Yet partner has inexplicably led a minor and from a short suit as well. Partner has thrown a touchdown pass and won't be happy if you drop the ball.

Ask Yourself
1. Where's the ♣Jack?
2. If you can establish clubs, where's your entry?
3. Could partner have an entry?
4. If partner is able to gain the lead, what would you like led?
5. How can you put the wheels in motion?

Dummy

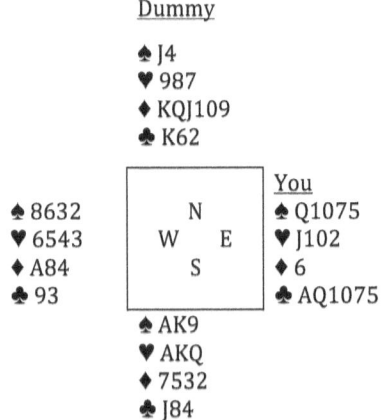

♠ J4
♥ 987
♦ KQJ109
♣ K62

```
♠ 8632      N       ♠ Q1075
♥ 6543   W     E    ♥ J102
♦ A84       S       ♦ 6
♣ 93                ♣ AQ1075
```

♠ AK9
♥ AKQ
♦ 7532
♣ J84

Answers
1. Declarer has the ♣Jack. There is no possible combination from which the 9 would be led from J/9.
2. Your only possible entry is clubs themselves.
3. Even if opener has a full 17 pts., partner could still have 4 pts. If you're lucky those 4 pts. could be an Ace.
4. Another club lead would be nice.
5. You can get your plan underway by ducking the opening lead but showing an interest in continuation at the same time. Play your 10.

When partner gets in with the ♦Ace, another club lead gets the defence 4 clubs. Along with partner's Ace that's a well-earned result.

40. Once Again, Any Port

♠ KQ2
♥ 653
♦ K109
♣ A1042

```
        ┌───────────┐ You
        │     N     │ ♠ A4
        │  W     E  │ ♥ 109872
        │     S     │ ♦ A85
        │           │ ♣ 753
        └───────────┘
```

E/W Vul.

West	North	East	South
---	---	---	1N.T.
P	3N.T.		

Opening Lead: ♠Jack

The Queen is played from dummy
and you win your Ace.

Ask Yourself

1. Should you return a spade?
2. What will happen if you do lead a spade?
3. Does partner have an entry?
4. If you decide not to lead a spade, what should you lead?
5. What is the most likely scenario if you do lead that card?

Dummy

♠ KQ2
♥ 653
♦ K109
♣ A1042

```
♠ J10973  ┌───────────┐ You
♥ KJ4     │     N     │ ♠ A4
♦ 743     │  W     E  │ ♥ 109872
♣ 86      │     S     │ ♦ A85
          └───────────┘ ♣ 753
            ♠ 865
            ♥ AQ
            ♦ QJ62
            ♣ KQJ9
```

Answers

1. Returning a spade would be the correct play if you had a third one which you could lead after winning your ♦Ace. Since you don't have a third one, returning a spade would be futile.
2. & 3. If you return a spade, declarer will likely run for home with that spade, 4 clubs, 3 diamonds and the ♥Ace which declarer must have to have the count for a N.T. opening.
4. & 5. You must lead the ♥10. If declarer plays the Ace, partner must begin the unblocking process

by dropping the Jack. Now, when you win your ♦Ace, you can lead to partner's
♥King and partner can lead the 4, enabling you to win 3 heart tricks for down 2.
And if declarer had tried the finesse when you led the 10, you'd still get all the tricks
to which you were entitled but in a different order.

41. Lots To Say

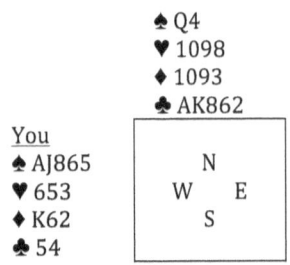

♠ Q4
♥ 1098
♦ 1093
♣ AK862

You
♠ AJ865
♥ 653
♦ K62
♣ 54

N/S Vul.

West	North	East	South
---	---	---	1N.T.
P	3N.T.		

Opening Lead: ♠6

Dummy plays the Queen and partner the 3*. This shows an odd number of cards which must be 3. If partner had 5, declarer would have a singleton, impossible with a N.T. opener. Declarer then runs the ♦10 to your King, partner playing the 7*.

Ask Yourself

1. Is there any future in continuing spades?
2. What if partner led spades?
3. How do you get to partner's hand?
4. Which card, in that suit, should you be leading?
5. How do you see the play proceeding if you follow this defence?
   *When giving a count signal, a high card played, indicates an even number of cards held in the suit while a low one shows an odd number.

Dummy

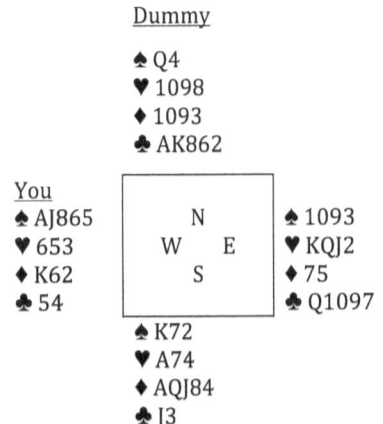

♠ Q4
♥ 1098
♦ 1093
♣ AK862

You
♠ AJ865
♥ 653
♦ K62
♣ 54

East
♠ 1093
♥ KQJ2
♦ 75
♣ Q1097

South
♠ K72
♥ A74
♦ AQJ84
♣ J3

Answers

1. Declarer obviously has the ♠King – partner didn't cover the Queen. Leading another spade would be tantamount to surrender.
2. A spade lead from partner would be exactly what the doctor ordered.
3. Only hearts offer any hope.
4. When leading hearts it must be the 6, top of nothing.
5. Declarer cannot allow partner to gain the lead, so will win with the Ace. Now that Declarer's ♥Ace has been dislodged, partner will

eventually gain the lead with a heart or club and lead a spade through the King. Declarer will be held to 8 tricks. H.C.P. are reasonably accurate in predicting how many tricks a hand will take. Perhaps North should only have raised to 2N.T. But those clubs made 3N.T. too tempting. You can be sure declarer would have passed 2.

42. Something Special

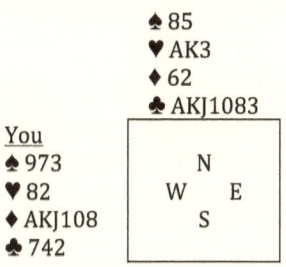

♠ 85
♥ AK3
♦ 62
♣ AKJ1083

You
♠ 973
♥ 82
♦ AKJ108
♣ 742

N
W E
S

E/W Vul.

West	North	East	South
---	1♣	P	1♥
P	3♣	P	3N.T.

Opening Lead: ♦Ace*

You lead the Ace, the 2, 4 and 3 are played in that order.
*When partner leads an Ace against 3N.T. your first obligation is to drop an honour if you have one. If you don't have one, your second obligation is to give count.

Ask Yourself

1. Where's the ♦Queen?
2. How many diamonds does partner have? Declarer?
3. How many points does declarer have? Partner?
4. Which is the only suit which could be an entry for partner?
5. Which card should you lead from that suit?

Dummy

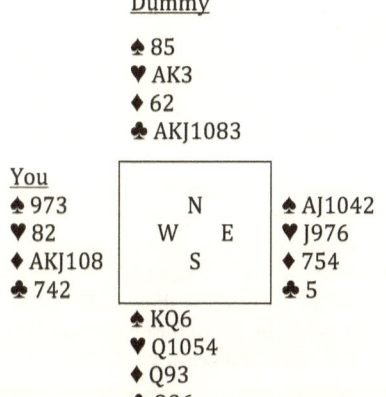

♠ 85
♥ AK3
♦ 62
♣ AKJ1083

You
♠ 973
♥ 82
♦ AKJ108
♣ 742

N
W E
S

♠ AJ1042
♥ J976
♦ 754
♣ 5

♠ KQ6
♥ Q1054
♦ Q93
♣ Q96

Answers

1. Partner didn't play it on trick #1, so declarer must have it.
2. Partner played a low card on the opening lead indicating an odd number. It must be 3. If partner had 5, declarer would have a singleton. Impossible, having shown a balanced hand.
3. Declarer bid 3N.T. after partner showed 16 or 17. Therefore declarer has around 10. That leaves partner with approximately 5.
4. Hearts and clubs are solid in dummy and you control the diamonds. It must be spades.
5. Lead the 9, top of nothing which helps partner read the suit. It also indicates no interest in having the spades returned. After winning the spade, partner will return a diamond, down 2.

43. What's The Distribution?

♠ J98432
♥ K3
♦ KJ4
♣ 75

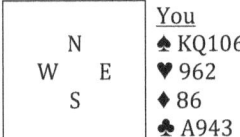

	You
N	♠ KQ106
W E	♥ 962
S	♦ 86
	♣ A943

Neither Vul.

West	North	East	South
---	---	---	1♥
P	1♠	P	3♦
P	3♠	P	3N.T.

Opening Lead: ♣2

For those who marvel at an experienced player's ability to determine an opponent's distribution, this hand is a good lesson and reveals how clues from the bidding and opening lead are utilized in this process. You win trick #1 with your Ace.

Ask Yourself
1. How many clubs does partner have?
2. How many hearts and diamonds does declarer have?
3. How many clubs and spades in declarer's hand?
4. What suit should you lead to trick #2?
5. Which card in that suit?

Dummy

♠ J98432
♥ K3
♦ KJ4
♣ 75

♠ A5			You
♥ 1085	N		♠ KQ106
♦ 10975	W E		♥ 962
♣ J1082	S		♦ 86
			♣ A943

♠ 9
♥ AQJ74
♦ AQ32
♣ KQ6

Answers
1. Partner led the ♣2. If it is fourth highest there are exactly 4 clubs in partner's hand. The 2 is the lowest card so partner can't have 5.
2. Declarer's bidding indicated 5 hearts and 4 diamonds.
3. Because partner has 4 clubs, declarer has 3. Because declarer has 5 hearts and 4 diamonds, there can only be room for one spade.
4. Only spades offer any hope for success.
5. You must lead the ♠6 so as to retain a tenace of the KQ10 over

dummy's Jack. You know partner has 2 spades. Hopefully one of them is the Ace.

44. A Little Deception

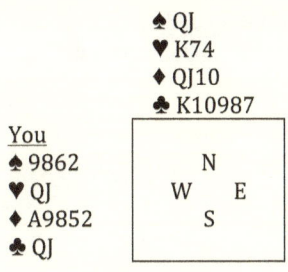

♠ QJ
♥ K74
♦ QJ10
♣ K10987

You
♠ 9862
♥ QJ
♦ A9852
♣ QJ

N
W   E
S

Both Vul.

West	North	East	South
---	---	---	1♥
P	2♣	P	2♠
P	3♥	P	3♠
P	4♥		

Opening Lead: ♣Queen

Dummy covers your opening lead and partner takes the Ace. With declarer having shown 6 hearts and 5 spades in the bidding and a club on the first trick, what was declarer's 13th card. Believing it to be a diamond, partner leads the 3 and you take your Ace.

Ask Yourself

1. How in the world can you get any more tricks?
2. Why not combine a little deception with a trump promotion?

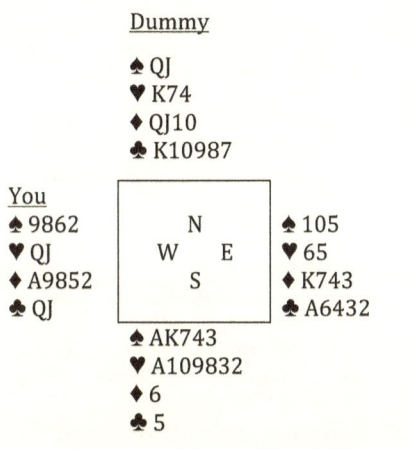

Dummy

♠ QJ
♥ K74
♦ QJ10
♣ K10987

You
♠ 9862
♥ QJ
♦ A9852
♣ QJ

N
W   E
S

♠ 105
♥ 65
♦ K743
♣ A6432

♠ AK743
♥ A109832
♦ 6
♣ 5

Answers

1. Your task sure looks hopeless.
2. If declarer is allowed to proceed in a normal fashion, holding 9 trump to the A/K, declarer will play for the drop of the trump Queen. Why not give declarer something to think about? Lead the trump Jack, looking like someone who has never seen a Queen. If declarer takes the bait, your Jack will be taken by dummy's King and partner will be finessed for the Queen. This will hold declarer to 10 tricks, no mean feat. If this was a pair's game,

where other declarer's were making 11 tricks with the same cards, you will have earned yourself a well-deserved top.

45. What Will Declarer Do?

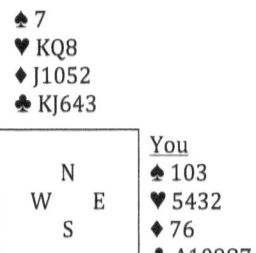

♠ 7
♥ KQ8
♦ J1052
♣ KJ643

You
♠ 103
♥ 5432
♦ 76
♣ A10987

Your echo in diamonds gets your side the first 3 tricks. Well, what now?

Both Vul.

West	North	East	South
---	---	---	1♠
P	2♣	P	2♥
P	3♥	P	4♥

Opening Lead: ♦Ace

Ask Yourself
1. What is declarer's distribution?
2. Needing all of the remaining tricks, what is declarer's likely course of action?
3. How can you upset declarer's applecart?

Dummy

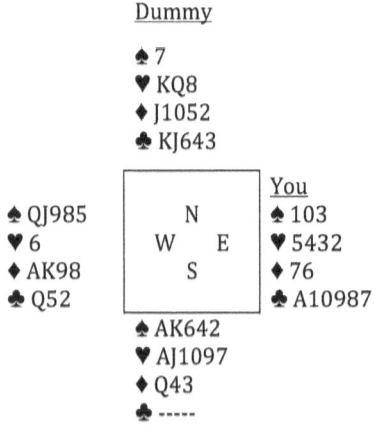

♠ 7
♥ KQ8
♦ J1052
♣ KJ643

♠ QJ985
♥ 6
♦ AK98
♣ Q52

You
♠ 103
♥ 5432
♦ 76
♣ A10987

♠ AK642
♥ AJ1097
♦ Q43
♣ -----

Answers

1. Declarer's bidding has revealed two 5 card majors. Having followed to 3 diamonds, declarer must be void in clubs.
2. The air has the unmistakable odour of a cross-ruff.
3. The counter-measure to a cross-ruff is a trump lead. If left unmolested, declarer's 10 tricks will consist of the 2 top spades, 3 spade ruffs in dummy and 5 club ruffs in hand. A trump lead will eliminate 2 of those ruffs. Defenders don't lead trump often enough. Sometimes a trump lead can be passive, trying to avoid a less palatable lead or it can serve a purpose as in this hand. In another book, by this author, the reader can find a list of 17 times when leading trump at the get-go is advantageous to the defence but only 4 where it would be a losing strategy. Overwhelming odds, n'est pas.

46. No Choice

```
        ♠ AK743
        ♥ Q6
        ♦ 432
        ♣ K87

You
♠ 109        N
♥ K42      W   E
♦ AJ85       S
♣ QJ109
```

Declarer wins the opening lead in dummy and immediately runs the ♥Queen to your King? What now, Batman?

N/S Vul.

West	North	East	South
---	---	---	1♥
P	1♠	P	2♥
P	4♥		

Opening Lead: ♣Queen

Ask Yourself
1. Who has the ♣Ace?
2. How many points in declarer's hand?
3. What does that leave for partner?
4. What suit offers some hope?
5. What card should you lead in that suit?

Dummy

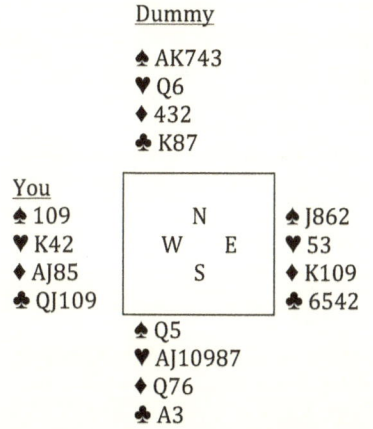

```
        ♠ AK743
        ♥ Q6
        ♦ 432
        ♣ K87

You                      ♠ J862
♠ 109        N           ♥ 53
♥ K42      W   E         ♦ K109
♦ AJ85       S           ♣ 6542
♣ QJ109
        ♠ Q5
        ♥ AJ10987
        ♦ Q76
        ♣ A3
```

Answers
1. Partner would have covered the King if he had the Ace. Declarer must have it.
2. Declarer rebid the hearts showing 6 cards and a minimum opening of 12 to 14.
3. Partner is very unlikely to have more than 3 or 4 pts.
4. The only hope must be diamonds. If this is your lucky day, partner's measly point count will include the ♦King.
5. By leading a low spot (the ♦5), partner will know that you have an

honour. By doing so, you've retained a tenace over declarer. When partner wins the ♦King and returns the 10, your well-reasoned defence will have paid dividends.

47. Hitch Your Wagon

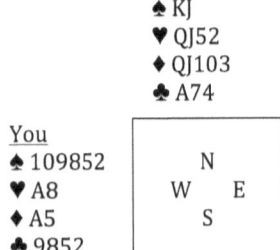

♠ KJ
♥ QJ52
♦ QJ103
♣ A74

You
♠ 109852
♥ A8
♦ A5
♣ 9852

N
W   E
S

*Jacoby 2N.T. – game going values and at least 4 trump.

Declarer wins trick #1 with dummy's Jack, partner playing the 4 and declarer the 3. Dummy now leads a heart which your win with the Ace.

N/S Vul.

West	North	East	South
---	---	---	1♥
P	2N.T.*	P	4♥

Opening Lead: ♠10

Ask Yourself
1. What do you know about spades?
2. What do you know about declarer's hand?
3. How many points does partner have and where?
4. To what suit do you hitch your wagon?

Dummy

♠ KJ
♥ QJ52
♦ QJ103
♣ A74

You
♠ 109852
♥ A8
♦ A5
♣ 9852

N
W   E
S

East
♠ 764
♥ 73
♦ K642
♣ QJ63

South
♠ AQ3
♥ K10964
♦ 987
♣ K2

Answers

1. When you can't win a trick in 3rd seat, giving count is the accepted wisdom. Partner's 4 on the first trick indicates an odd number – here it can only be 3. Declarer also has 3, the AQ3.
2. It is a minimum opening bid and balanced. In response to Jacoby 2N.T., opener can bid a singleton at the 3 level or show another 5 card suit by bidding 4 of it.
3. You have 8 pts., dummy has 14 and declarer about 13. Partner cannot have any more than 6 and those pts. must be in the minor suits.
4. With a little bit of luck, the ♦King will be part of those 6 pts. Lead you ♦Ace, followed by the 5. Your side will get the 2 red Aces, the ♦King and a diamond ruff.

48. You Need One More

♠ Q1087
♥ K109
♦ K98
♣ 743

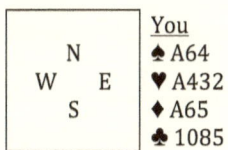

You
♠ A64
♥ A432
♦ A65
♣ 1085

E/W Vul.

West	North	East	South
---	---	---	1N.T.
P	2♣	P	2♠
P	3♠	P	4♠

Opening Lead: ♦7

Partner's opening lead could be any one of these 4 holdings – 742, 74, 72 or a singleton. Hoping that it is a singleton or doubleton, you win your Ace and return the suit.

Ask Yourself
1. Where is your fourth trick?
2. How many trump does partner have?
3. How do you see the defence proceeding?

Dummy

♠ Q1087
♥ K109
♦ K98
♣ 743

♠ 53
♥ 8765
♦ 72
♣ QJ962

You
♠ A64
♥ A432
♦ A65
♣ 1085

♠ KJ92
♥ QJ
♦ QJ104
♣ AK3

Answers

1. Your fourth trick might come from a diamond ruff if partner has 2 diamonds at most and more than one trump.
2. Declarer's bidding has shown 4 trump, dummy has 4 and you have 3. Partner must have 2.
3. You've already taken the first trick and returned the suit. When declarer leads trump, take your Ace immediately and lead a third diamond. Partner's ruff and your 3 Aces will be 4 tricks. You'll then hear your opponent's be moaning their bad luck in encountering such a stellar defence.

111

49. Grasping At Straws

♠ Q109
♥ QJ10
♦ QJ732
♣ J10

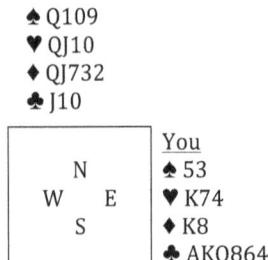

	You
	♠ 53
W E	♥ K74
S	♦ K8
	♣ AKQ864

You take the opening lead with the Queen. Now what?

E/W Vul.

West	North	East	South
---	---	1♣	1♠
2♣	2♠	3♣	4♠

Opening Lead: ♣7

Ask Yourself
1. Is declarer likely to have more clubs?
2. Where are declarer's points?
3. How do you feel about your red Kings?
4. Can you see any other tricks in addition to the first one?

Dummy

♠ Q109
♥ QJ10
♦ QJ732
♣ J10

♠ 74	N	You
♥ 9842	W E	♠ 53
♦ A109	S	♥ K74
♣ 9752		♦ K8
		♣ AKQ864

♠ AKJ862
♥ A63
♦ 654
♣ 3

Answers
1. Partner raised your minor suit and must have at least 4, so declarer's 3 has to be a singleton.
2. Declarer's points have to be all the unseen spade honours and one or both red Aces.
3. One or both of your red Kings are in jeopardy.
4. Your only hope is that partner has the ♦Ace. Having the ♥Ace wouldn't do you any good because you'd get 2 heart tricks at most. Lead your ♦King in hopes of getting a diamond ruff. Your tricks would then consist of the ♣Ace, the top diamond honours and a diamond ruff.

50.   Rule Of Eleven

♠ 542
♥ A4
♦ KJ873
♣ A109

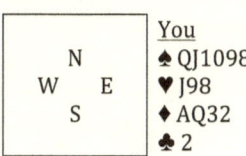

```
        N        You
                 ♠ QJ1098
    W       E    ♥ J98
        S        ♦ AQ32
                 ♣ 2
```

N/S Vul.

West	North	East	South
---	---	---	1N.T.
P	3N.T.		

Opening Lead: ♥3

On the opening lead, your Jack loses to declarer's Queen. Now declarer leads the ♦10 and you win the Queen as partner discards the ♣3. Should you lead spades or hearts.

Ask Yourself

1. What is partner's distribution?
2. Does declarer have any other heart stopper?
3. Where are the top spades?
4. Which other honours does declarer have?
5. If you lead a spade, after taking trick #2, how many tricks will declarer get?
6. If you return partner's suit instead, how many tricks will declarer get?

Dummy

♠ 542
♥ A4
♦ KJ873
♣ A109

```
♠ 763        N        You
♥ K10632             ♠ QJ1098
♦ -----  W       E   ♥ J98
♣ 87643      S       ♦ AQ32
                     ♣ 2
        ♠ AK
        ♥ Q75
        ♦ 10964
        ♣ KQJ5
```

Answers

1. First discards are normally from 5 card suits and partner is void in diamonds. Partner's opening lead was probably from a 5 card suit, so partner would seem to be 3 – 5 – 0 – 5.
2. The Rule of Eleven disclosed that declarer has no more heart stoppers.
3. & 4. Declarer must have the Ace and King of spades and the KQJ of clubs to have opened 1N.T.
5. If you lead a spade, declarer will

win, play another diamond and get home with 2 spades, 2 hearts, 3 diamonds and 4 clubs for 11 tricks.
6. If you lead a heart and then another one when you win a second diamond, declarer will win 2 spades, 2 hearts and 4 clubs for only 8 tricks.

www.ingramcontent.com/pod-product-compliance
Lightning Source LLC
Chambersburg PA
CBHW020539290526
45786CB00002B/963